PRODUCT LIABILITY

LIABILITY
A Management Response

PRODUCT LIABILITY
A Management Response

IRWIN GRAY
with

Albert L. Bases Charles H. Martin
Alexander Sternberg

amacom
A division of
American Management Associations

```
Library of Congress Cataloging in Publication Data

Gray, Irwin
   Product liability.

   Includes bibliographical references and index.
   1. Products liability—United States. I. Title.
KF1296.G7         346'.73'038         75-1261
ISBN  0-8144-5373-2
```

© 1975 AMACOM
A division of American Management Associations, New York.
All rights reserved. Printed in the United States of America.

Second Printing

TO HESTER

PREFACE

The trend toward selecting attorneys as high corporate officers and the explosive growth of in-house legal staffs are symptomatic of the problems confronting business. New branches of the law are created every day: Ecology, civil rights, affirmative action, and product liability are just a few that the corporation must respond to.

Many of these trends will affect all firms to a reasonably equal degree or, what is most important to the manager, will increase his competitor's costs pretty much to the degree they inflate his own. A major exception is the cost of consumerism—particularly product liability lawsuits. These suits are not likely to fall equally on all competitors; rather, they will fall more on firms that acquire a reputation as good lawsuit targets because of brand prominence, product type, firm size, or plain carelessness in responding to a suit.

It is the normal course of business for a manager to enlarge and enhance brand prominence and firm size. But it is dangerous business to make an inadequate response to a product liability lawsuit. Money and reputation losses are cumulative. Trial attorneys trade information and techniques. They penetrate the coffers of the firm's insurance company; the insurance company in turn penetrates the coffers of the firm through increased deductibles, exclusions, or denial of coverage entirely.

Usually the conduct of a liability suit is placed under the direction of an in-house or insurer's attorney, and the firm's officers need only respond appropriately to his direct questions and orders. The attorney calls on people as he needs them, carries on the case, brings it to a conclusion, presents the bills (most often to the insurance carrier), and fades out of the picture. The attorney cautions everyone concerned to be more "watchful" and business proceeds as usual. The net amount learned from the painful lesson may be very little or nothing—especially if the insurance company and the corporate tax mechanism have effectively diluted the financial impact. Usually it is the sad truth that except for the people directly involved in the suit, no one in the firm even learns about it. It is treated as dirty linen—to be kept buried in the firm's files and expunged from the corporate conscience. Possible corrections to the product often stay buried as well.

Consider the experience of dealing with illness. Tests are taken, doctors and nurses perform their duties, and the patient gets well. The patient and his family, however, rarely learn anything about what has really transpired in the course of the illness beyond the cost when the bills come in. Here there is usually no harm done by the knowledge not gained, because recurrence is unlikely. With product liability this is not so. The product-based accident can recur simply because the firm failed to learn from prior cases; the attorney for the injured party will introduce previous cases in court, thereby embarrassing the firm and enhancing its guilt.

This book is addressed to the firm which has been (or might in the future be) hit by a product liability suit. Management should learn everything that can happen in the course of such a suit and, not incidentally, how to avoid a repetition. To continue with the medical analogy, this book considers the onset of a disease striking the firm (the product liability suit), the role of the doctors (the corporate and insurance attorneys), the medicines the firm uses to assuage the effects of the disease (the insurance carried for the coverage of liability suits), and the therapy for full recovery and prevention of future attacks (product liability prevention procedures).

The principal author, researcher, and writer for this book is Irwin Gray, who has the dual interests of engineering and management. As an engineer he acts as a product-liability-prevention consultant to corporations and as an expert witness in the courtroom for both defendant and plaintiff attorneys. His management interests include a teaching position as a Professor of Business Management at the City University of New York and a consulting practice to industry and government in policy planning and managerial behavior. The three coauthors contributed substantial material in the form of notes, interviews, private papers, document collections, and appropriate rewrites of drafts of the manuscript. Albert L. Bases is a trial lawyer with extensive experience in defending and prosecuting product liability suits. Charles H. Martin is an experienced risk manager who spent twenty years with a giant chemicals firm and is now an independent consultant for trade associations and firms. And Alexander Sternberg is an independent consultant who has extensive experience in helping firms set up product liability/quality control systems that enhance product quality and will hold up in court.

The book's organization is as follows: In the first chapter we trace the evolution of product liability laws. In the next three chapters we cover the litigation process, from the first receipt of a claim to resolution by a jury. In Chapter 5 we cover the role of insurance and its declining ability to buffer the firm against the financial blows of liability cases. In Chapter 6 we discuss product liability prevention with what we hope is a practical, down-to-earth approach. And in Chapter 7 we offer some thoughts for the future and a review of the book's major points.

We hope this book will enjoy multifaceted use. For attorneys it will serve as a checklist of the procedures involved in prosecuting or defending a lawsuit. It provides a guide to the use of the expert witness, as well as a guide to the responsibilities of companies faced with product liability claims. Managers involved in a suit will, we hope, better understand just what happens in the course of a suit, their role in defending against a suit, and how to act to forestall mistakes. Risk managers can use this book to evaluate whether they are buying the correct kind and amount of coverage for their firm. Finally, we hope the book will guide top management in building a comprehensive product liability prevention system tailored to the needs of its firm and its products. We have tried to make the steps in preventing liability detailed enough so that the various functions in the firm can assume their proper roles in liability prevention, and broad enough so that top management can ask the right questions about its overall approach.

The principal author extends his thanks to several people. First, to Melvin Maiman, attorney, for contributing comprehensive background information about the evolution and operation of laws concerning product liability. Second, to Edward D. Goldberg, who provided insightful analyses of how organizations react to crises and why they need the type of programs we cover in Chapter 7 under "Continuously Prepare for Liability." Third and fourth, but in no particular order, thanks go to Isidore R. Tucker, attorney, and Ray M. S. Tucker, attorney, for their background comments and advice. Fifth, the author wishes to thank attorney Joseph Kelner, who taught him the basics of product liability law, how to be an expert witness, and what the word "preparedness" means in winning a case. And finally, thanks go to attorney Warren Eginton, who was never too busy to answer a question or provide a piece of source material.

—*The Authors*

CONTENTS

1

INTRODUCTION

Many corporate executives consider product liability a matter that rests at their attorneys' door. These executives are using a tourniquet to stem a serious profit hemorrhage—and in many cases the tourniquet is not going to hold.

The hemorrhage is not inevitable. An effective preventive is imaginative policy making at the top executive levels and careful assignment of liability prevention to operating groups. In fact, top executive action is the sine qua non of comprehensive product liability prevention.

There is reason to believe that several potent forces will fuel the constant expansion of product liability suits. Most executives are aware of the efforts of government agencies, consumer groups, and other consumer protectors to create a climate in which the firm which produced a product is responsible for its mishaps—a climate of "automatic corporate liability" regardless of the negligence involved. But the real threat to profits does not come from these climate creators; pressure from them can be avoided at reasonable cost by diligence and ingenuity in the product design and production processes. The real threat comes from those attorneys who see companies as bottomless wells from which to compensate people who have any kind of accident involving a product—who see the manufacturer as best able to absorb the immediate injury costs because the loss can later be recovered through the price mechanism.[1]

Not too long ago, product liability suits were a rarity, and this worked to the advantage of manufacturers. Attorneys tend to deal with familiar things and shy away from aspects of law that are unfamiliar to them. Auto cases, for example, are common; the expenses incurred in pursuing such cases are minimal, and filing and court procedures are familiar and accepted. Product liability cases, on the other hand, have been beyond the scope of practice of most attorneys. Although reams of material[2] are published to familiarize attorneys with the disposition of such cases, few attorneys have had a real motivation to shift to this new line of law. There has also been an even greater stumbling block: Before a case in product liability can even be started, a professional engineering consultant generally must be engaged. The amounts of money charged for his services are not insignificant, and the injured client must be convinced to make the investment. The attorney runs a high risk that the consultant will find the claim is baseless, and a negative report for the client generally means an unhappy client.

So, many attorneys turn down product liability cases, neglect them, or file briefs that are unsupported by engineering evidence and poorly written. These cases are obviously being pursued for their nuisance value; volume and low expenditure of time are compensation for the relatively low return. The opportunity cost to the client may or may not be high, depending on how defective the product really was. But the effect on the manufacturer is relatively low claim-settlement costs.

This "fine"state of affairs is not due to last. The law schools are graduating specialists in product liability law, attorneys are taking update-seminars, and universal no-fault automobile insurance will restrict legal practice in that area.*

---

* At this writing, 21 states already have their own plans, and there is a public clamor for no-fault auto insurance on a national level. It is now recognized that even the unfortunate victims are not served by our current system. A 1970 *New York Times* article noted that auto accident

The present consumer-oriented climate favors these trends. The consumer is, by and large, convinced that the products he buys today are not as good as those he bought yesterday. He senses he is the goat for companies that simply don't care or are negligent in quality control. He feels more and more that he is not only the *final* inspector of the product but the *only* inspector of the product. He is demanding legislative protection and is more aware that he can redress his grievances by instituting legal action against the people who made, distributed, and sold the product which displeased him. It follows that the legal profession and its clients will make increasing use of consulting engineers to examine the firm's product and will become more accustomed to the expenses and procedures involved in finding out whether a firm can be the target of a lawsuit.

The changing climate is illustrated by the following impressive array of organizations that are ready to chastise the manufacturer:

1. Independent research groups, such as Consumers Union.
2. Federal, state, and local consumer buying groups.
3. Federal, state, and local government agencies.
4. Industrywide self-regulatory agencies.*
5. University researchers.
6. Serious consumer advocates, such as Ralph Nader, who publicly attack industry for its lack of social responsibility in product safety.
7. Competing firms.
8. The general consensus of society (as reflected in the decisions of judges and juries).
9. Trained, independent consultants—the "defect hunters."

---

victims recover less than one-fifth of their losses from auto insurance companies. With disability payments, medical benefits, and social security payments, they altogether recoup only one-half of their losses.[3]

* Some examples of outstanding association programs are listed in *FDA Papers*, September 1969, p. 11. Examples are the programs of the American Baking Institute and the National Paint and Coatings Association. In industries where an association issues adequate standards and obtains compliance, FDA seldom finds it necessary to take legal action.

Item 7 is of particular interest, as many executives find it difficult to believe that a competitor would subject them to a liability suit. They do not do so intentionally; rather, competing firms provide sales literature and supporting materials to show why their product is better than others on the market. One can sometimes piece together quite a bit of intelligence about a firm's poor design simply by examining how the competitors successfully guarded against defects or provided safety features.

Item 9 is interesting too. A reasonably conscientious consultant can collect an enormous amount of information on almost any subject and on almost any product. With this information base he can seek out defects in the product and expose the firm to a product liability suit. With this array lined up against it, the firm is well advised to consider where, exactly, it is vulnerable.

AREAS OF CORPORATE VULNERABILITY

A survey of court reports in which *Fortune* 500 firms were involved revealed the following sample of plaintiff allegations: [4]

1. Defective construction or materials.
2. Failure to comply with codes.
3. Failure to investigate the sciences.
4. Failure to properly warn the user of hazards.
5. Failure of the product to perform as advertised.
6. Improper design.
7. Failure fault of two or more manufacturers.

The plaintiff attorneys based their cases on breach of warranty, strict liability in tort, and negligence on the part of all those who put the product line into the stream of commerce. We will forgo discussion of these terms until a later section in this chapter, in which a logical development of the law is presented. For now, it will be worthwhile to expand on items 2, 3, and 7 above, as these are frequently confusing.

Failure to comply with codes, item 2, is illustrated by the manufacturer who attached to his products, intentionally or unintentionally, an Underwriters' Laboratories seal that applied to his lamp wire but not the entire lamp. The latter may have been perfectly suitable for its intended use, but to the potential consumer it appeared that the seal covered the entire product. To avoid this kind of confusion, Underwriters' Laboratories moved some time ago to prevent use of the seal on wires alone. The point is that some firms intentionally produce a cheaper item—which could not pass a code—and use a cover seal to make it appear as if the entire product is covered. Courts of law have virtually no sympathy for this practice.

Item 3, failure to investigate the sciences, is especially pertinent in view of the growing concern with the environment. A firm producing atomic-electric power may innocently think it has covered all liability problems by maintaining adequate radiation controls when suddenly it finds itself the target of a fisherman's lawsuit for fish killed due to thermal pollution. The engineers for the firm should have been aware of all aspects of their activities. They should have realized that the plant's cooling water discharge was too hot for the fish in the receiving body of water, but engineers generally do not read outside their immediate field. In a casual survey made of engineering students in ten different graduate courses, virtually no students made any concerted effort to read in the sciences allied to their own. They depended, for the most part, on the technical journal in their immediate field to call attention to allied developments. In fact, for a large number (over 80 percent) of these students, the reading of *any* kind of journal was not a regular affair; it was hit or miss, depending on a fortuitous combination of available time and available reading material.[5]

Finally, item 7, the failure fault of two or more manufacturers, is best illustrated by the sequence of events that followed Apollo 13's explosion in space. The final reports of the investigating committee stated that the explosion of the oxygen tanks and fuel supplies was caused by failure to change a switch (by one company), failure to check for the changes (by a second company), over-voltage testing (by a third company), and NASA's failure to look into pre-launch problems when the tanks gave some indication of probable deficiencies. In a product liability case, each firm would find itself involved regardless of its particular proportion of blame.

MANAGEMENT'S RESPONSE

Over the past two decades, management's response to product liability may be likened to the response of a blinded giant to the pinpricks of Lilliputians. In this case the giant has flailed in all directions, has had some small successes, has established some areas of strength, and has attempted to gain allies; but its actions on a day-to-day level remain uncoordinated. Responses to consumer claims have ranged from sending detectives after Ralph Nader to settling out of court just to avoid publicity, even when the damage claims were patently false and irresponsible.

Here are some of the directions that firms have explored in attempts to protect themselves. On a macro (nationwide or industrywide) level, they have:

1. Intensified their lobbying to kill off consumer protection legislation or weaken existing agencies.
2. Set up manufacturers' captive organizations to perform "independent" testing or guaranteeing of merchandise.
3. Enhanced their legal defenses by working closely with the Defense Research Institute, which provides help in locating expert witnesses, publishes material for management and defense attorneys, and helps members locate useful publications and records.
4. Established national standards organizations.
5. Adopted federal or state agency standards as performance minimums.
6. Made increasing use of independent laboratory certifications, such as those of Underwriters' Laboratories.
7. Adopted the standards of national societies such as the American Society of Mechanical Engineers, the American Society for Quality Control, and the Institute of Electrical and Electronics Engineers.

On a micro or individual firm level, they have tried:

8. Tightening up advertising.
9. Tightening up design.
10. Keeping a tighter watch over manufacturing methods and personnel.
11. Better quality control.
12. More insurance.
13. Expanding and improving their legal staff.
14. A risk management function.
15. An "independent corporate-level safety watchdog committee." [6]
16. An independent consultant.

Is the lineup impressive? Probably so, but with the possible exception of the risk manager or the emerging corporate safety committee (the latter might range in composition and scope from a periodic executive-level discussion group to a hazards-analysis and design-review team), in most firms there is no agency that coordinates these 16 items. In an individual case where a large amount of money is at stake, the insurance company may call in an independent consultant who is given the authority to roam the company checking on items 8 through 15 and to examine all sources for information on items 1 through 7. It is rare indeed, however, to see this blanket examination conducted before the difficulties are encountered.

Many managers are inclined to underestimate the "attacking forces" and overestimate their own defense forces. But consider the various arrays on each side of the fence. Earlier in this chapter we listed seven areas of company vulnerability and nine types of agencies seeking to work against the firm. Since each of the nine agencies can attack any or all of the seven areas of vulnerability, the firm is open to attack on 63 different fronts. The company is in somewhat the same situation as a large army subjected to guerrilla attacks. The guerrillas choose the time, the place, and the vehicle for their activities while the army must prepare all-around defense.

The effects of guerrilla attacks on an army can be devastating; the effects of product liability attacks on an organization are even more so. First the insurance costs rise, then exclusion clauses in the contracts grow more enveloping, and finally the firm is forced either to absorb losses from current earnings (no insurance) or to set aside a highly liquid investment fund to cover expected losses (self-insurance). A series of small pinpricks on 63 different areas results, inevitably, in reduced profits.

THE COST-QUALITY-QUANTITY TRIANGLE

In order to fully understand the existing responses and actions of organizations exposed to product liability problems and to set the stage for some possible resolution of the dilemmas, let us examine the concept of a cost-quality-quantity triangle.

Visualize an equilateral triangle whose apexes represent the three concerns of a firm producing a product for profit. The first apex represents cost. One way in which a firm seeks to maximize profits is by reducing costs to the greatest extent possible. The second apex represents quantity. Number of units currently being sold, size of market, market penetration, and inventory policies strongly determine the extent to which management pushes for more or less quantity with given production facilities. The third apex represents quality. Unfortunately, there is no such thing as quality language; one cannot say a firm has reached a given number of "quals." Measurements of how well a firm's products are functioning or how safe they are tend to be based on negative concepts such as units rejected. Quality in a firm may be roughly translated to mean quality considerations in design, production, sales, and follow-up services.

Of the three concerns, quality is obviously the most relevant to product liability prevention.[7] Yet the cost of quality control is usually treated as overhead to the production function of the firm, and overhead is always a target for cost reduction. When a firm is concentrating on a particular concern—be it cost, quality, or quantity—the other two receive less attention. It may be said that the triangle rotates over time, with its orientation indicating the direction of corporate emphasis.

A product is usually designed to meet a specific market

need and priced to achieve a specific market penetration. Once price is set (whether by external forces or marketing considerations), the cost of the product becomes a relevant consideration: It must be kept low enough so that the rate of return on the targeted volume justifies the investment.[8] And these costs are expected to fall even lower as production gets underway. When cost becomes the main consideration, as is usually the case with a firm that has geared up to produce a "required" volume, the triangle may be visualized as revolving so that the cost apex is on top and the quantity and quality apexes on the bottom. In the consciousness of corporate executives, cost is uppermost.

As market penetration builds, however, quantity becomes a target. The increased volume a firm can build, even at a reduction in price, can often provide a healthy increase in the rate of return on the initial investment.[9] As management's accent on quantity builds, the triangle rotates to bring quantity up alongside cost. Quantity and cost now form the base of an inverted triangle. Unfortunately, the apex of quality has now lost a considerable degree of its stature, being relegated to a pronounced underdog position. Corporate executives who are geared to quality in production find that their desires are subordinated to those of executives who are geared to quantity, costs, and budgets.

The outside environment influences the triangle as well. Government agencies at all jurisdictional levels attempt to enforce quality standards. (The myriad pure food and drug acts and the Consumer Product Safety Act are the most notable examples of quality enforcement to protect the consumer.) Consumer groups and consumer protection agencies also affect the triangle. Their efforts are aimed at revolving the triangle so quality becomes uppermost.

Supervisors on the lower operating levels bear the brunt of poor product quality and consumer backlash. They transmit their problems up the line, but since resolution of their problems would result in added overhead as opposed to increased production, their requests are often in conflict with the major emphasis of the organization. Many times top management will attempt to resolve its problems by ostensibly flattening the triangle and placing quality on an equal level with the other considerations, or at least only slightly below them. But under the pressure to achieve tangible, measurable results in terms of dollars earned and production units achieved, the triangle soon reverts to the form in which quality is downgraded. The lower-level managers understandably react with misgivings, uncertainty, and slowed decision making.

Faced with these conflicting pressures, how then do top managers establish policy? They say: "Let our quality control people handle it."

QUALITY CONTROL: THE CIRCUMSCRIBED FUNCTION

A department charged with looking after quality may have any of several titles, depending on the ultimate customer of the organization's products. If the ultimate customer is the government—especially in Department of Defense contracting—quality control will be called Quality Assurance or Contract Compliance, or will have a similar title indicating the great stress on quality. If the ultimate customer is an industrial producer, the title is usually a variation of the above. But the consumer goods manufacturers, until the recent wave of publicity, were usually served by a Quality Control Department. Too often, these departments were severely restricted in size, scope, and depth and limited by their personnel's lack of professional self-image.

The role of quality control in establishing quality is severely circumscribed even before the product is born. In a survey of 109 presidents of top firms, the majority of executives expressed the belief that quality control departments know nothing about the marketing, management, and industrial psychology techniques necessary for the proper operation of a business.[10] In other words, top managers are of the opinion that their own watchdogs over quality cannot understand the other forces bearing on the triangle's rotation. As a result, they are certainly not likely to entrust to this department any coordination of the firm's efforts on a macro or micro level. Furthermore, the work that this department does is all too often channeled in an unimaginative fashion. It becomes mired in the technicalities of product sampling, defect recording, and other inspection-oriented activities, which prevents its personnel from attempting to act as coordinators on a broader basis.

It is significant to note how three very large firms responded to the call for safer products, as recorded in a *Business Week* article.[11] None of the firms made any mention of enlarging the role or enhancing the work of their quality control personnel. One firm reported it had set up a "corporate product safety committee," a second said it "watches its customers operate its products," and a third "sends products to a company test center." It can hardly be claimed that these nebulous "solutions" are cheaper than expanding the activities of an existing group of personnel already dealing with product defects and their ramifications on the assembly floor—unless the group has been judged incapable of performing anything other than a limited task.

What happens in an organization, therefore, when liability cases become of concern and there have been few provisions made for the role of quality control or for coordination of efforts? Experience with a number of firms indicates that the mainstay has been the firm's legal department and insurance underwriter—one of the most expensive solutions available. The services of attorneys, law firms, and attendant researchers in and out of house are far more expensive than those of in-house engineers, who might have been able to eliminate liability problems entirely if they had been given the chance originally. The average starting salary for an attorney is greater than the salary of all but a small minority of those in the quality control field. The work performed by the insurance company is eventually paid for by higher insurance fees, tougher exclusion clauses, and reduced coverage limits. The insurance company's legal staff performs the coordinating function or assigns it to an outside liability consultant. The work that the manufacturer or distributor neglected to do is finally done in preparation for a liability defense, but with the terrible disadvantage that it is done for a limited situation (response to a particular lawsuit) and for a limited time (until the case is closed). It is rare for any sort of comprehensive program to emerge and rarer still for top management to exert any policy efforts. "It can't happen here" reigned before; "it won't happen again" reigns afterwards.

IT CAN HAPPEN HERE

Vulnerability of the producer and distributor to claims caused by a defective product is rooted in commercial history and in law. Attorneys tend to point to "landmark" judicial decisions as having radically changed the degree of vulnerability, but examination of the change process reveals it to be evolutionary and not revolutionary.

Codes of law found in the remains of ancient kingdoms call attention to many problems similar to those we have today. Buyer and seller had a fairly easy time agreeing on price, quantity, and delivery date, but quality remained the source of much litigation before kings and their representatives. Particular difficulties were encountered in the sale of grain. A king's codes may have specified that the quality of the full shipment must match the quality of the sample, but how much of a sample was to be taken? How much deviation from the sample was to be allowed before the shipment had what we now call a "substantial deviation" and the contract for sale was voided? The law quickly recognized that inspection of an entire grain shipment, down to the individual grains, was impossible, and the element of "commercial integrity," with compensation for deviations, became an integral part of judicial decisions.

In medieval Europe, the same problem manifested itself in the textile industry. Here the workman was producing for his lord, who in turn would affix his seal to entire bales of cloth. The seal represented a quality mark, as no feudal lord would accept payment from his serf in shoddy goods,[12] so the purchaser did not have to unroll and inspect every piece of cloth. Recovery of damages for inferior quality was the accepted right of the lord and, through him, of the purchaser as well.

With the coming of guilds in the eleventh and twelfth centuries, the textile trade and the capital investment in it expanded as the number of links in the chain from raw material to finished product increased. Each craftsman performing an operation had to be paid as he completed his work, and cloth merchants arose to finance production until monies could be recovered from the ultimate consumer. The town governments also saw this trade as an opportunity for regulation and tax collection. As a result, it soon became "[in] the interest of both the entrepreneurs and magistrates to keep watch on the craftsmen they lent money to and protected, and to insure these produced first class goods." [13] Quality control became part of a series of regulations with political rather than economic aims.[14] By the twelfth century extensive controls had been instituted all over Europe, with mechanisms for levying and collecting fines.

Documents from thirteenth-century Germany stipulate punishment for falsification of fabrics,[15] which indicates that guilds and authorities had extensive inspection authority. By the fourteenth century, "officials descended on weavers' workshops at regular intervals to check cloth on the looms, to count warp ends in each piece, and to test weft yarns." [16] Leading merchants purchasing for resale also inspected the manufacturing centers and put their own seals on goods to gain a wide reputation for assuring the integrity of the goods they marketed.

The use of seals and stamps as quality indicators, especially in the form of metal tags affixed to merchandise, is thought by some to be related to the origin and use of money. When commerce shifted in Roman times from commodity exchange to metal, unstamped bars of copper were used, leading to difficulties in weighing and assaying them.[17] To prevent abuses, a public stamp was affixed upon certain quantities of particular metals. "Hence, the origin of coined money, and of those public offices called mints; institutions exactly of the same nature with those of the aulnagers (woolen cloth measures in England) and stampmasters (protectors against cloth debasement in the linen districts of Scotland) of woolen and linen cloth." [18]

The trademarks used by the modern textile industry to guarantee quality originated in Britain, where they found acceptance first in the wholesale trade and then, from the late 1800s on, among consumers.[19] As machines and processes were developed to maintain certain standards, the selection of raw materials, control of the production processes, and inspection of end products replaced the visit by the town inspector or merchant to the weaving center as the quality control mechanism. As control of raw materials and control of the production process were relied on more and more, the necessity of examining each square yard of cloth coming off the machine was reduced. Statistical quality control based on a sampling plan came into being.

Merchants came to accept registered trademarks as guarantees that adequate controls had been exercised from beginning to end of the production process. The type of contract law that the ancient kings used in buying grain was now an everyday practice in dealing with other types of merchandise: The merchants bought by sample and accepted the entire shipment if it was of substantially the same quality. The trademark was the assurance that there would be no deviations, or deviations not serious enough to cause rejection.

This background provides us with an understanding of modern-day legal defenses of sampling plans. We know it is not feasible, economically or otherwise, to examine every product coming into the chain of distribution. The economic reasons go back to the aforementioned textile merchants who accepted a feudal lord's seal because they could not afford the time and labor to unroll and inspect every bale of goods. The physical reasons go back to the impossibility of the grain merchants' examining every grain in the shipment. Today, as then, if a sample passes inspection and the rest of the shipment is made from the stock or components under the same process controls, then the merchant will accept the rest of the shipment. The manufacturer takes a similar approach to sampling from a process. If one sample of a lot failed, it may be that a metallic impurity was peculiar to that one sample; if further samples pass inspection, the entire lot will usually be accepted.

Legal defenses of sampling hinge, therefore, on acceptance of the idea that product sampling is akin to sampling grain shipments and that some failures will necessarily slip by at irregular intervals. To defend himself against charges made about his sampling plan, a manufacturer will try to demonstrate that (1) he could not examine every single item in production, for any of the aforementioned reasons; (2) he had a very good sampling plan—one that met all the criteria for statistical reliability and the highest professional standards; and (3) the unit that caused the accident was probably one of only an extremely small number that could have gotten through. If the manufacturer's argument is convincing, he may mitigate, or even destroy, the plaintiff's charge of negligence in manufacture. Since a charge of negligence carries a punitive value in the minds of most jurors, reducing or eliminating the force of this charge is a definite plus to the defense. The defendant manufacturer can still be charged with strict liability in tort (which we will define later in this chapter); the judge will inform the jury that the manufacturer is absolutely liable "because he let the defect pass through his processes and inspection system." However, the jurors may accept the fact that not every item that comes off the production line can be inspected and reason that there is a certain element of risk a person assumes in consuming or using a product. They may, and in many cases do, reject the charge and find for the defendant.

To further understand how the law works, we must examine how legal doctrines are developed. Anderson and Kumpf define law as "the entire body of principles that govern conduct and the observance of which can be enforced in courts." [20] *Statutory laws* are those adopted by legislative bodies. These bodies include Congress, state legislatures, and city legislatures or other subdivisions that have local jurisdiction. *Administrative regulations* are those promulgated by national and state administrative agencies and are part of the law governing all business activities. In addition to the above, there are common law and case law, which are developed through the courts. *Common law* (or community law) is a body of unwritten principles, recognized and enforced by the courts, based on customs and usages of the community.[21] Common law, which owes its origins to England and the centuries following the Norman Conquest in 1066, became the foundation of law in the American colonies. Its modern manifestations are the "principles and practices" of a trade, which are introduced by attorneys in a suit to explain ambiguities and guide courts in their decisions. *Case law* evolves from judicial decisions. Decisions on a new question or problem that involve principles expressed for the first time become precedents and stand as the law for that particular problem in the future.[22] The rule that a court decision becomes a precedent to be followed in similar cases is the doctrine of *stare decisis*.[23] The judge is, however, not absolutely bound by *stare decisis* and may find a new precedent in any case that comes before him.

Our discussion of quality has so far considered only economic damages. It should also be noted that "by the Middle Ages, fairly strict liability for injuries—without contract, misrepresentation, or evidence of negligence—was often the rule." [24]

By the mid-eighteenth century, however, there had been a change in society's view of business and its responsibilities to those it injured. The new view was expressed in the famous case of *Winterbottom v. Wright* [25] and in Adam Smith's "invisible hand" theory of commercial regulation.[26] In *Winterbottom,* a coach with a defective wheel overturned, and the injured passengers sued the coach operator and coach builder. The court absolved the party with the immediate contractual relationship to the passengers—the operator—of any blame as he did not know the wheel was defective. And the coach builder was held not to have had a contractual relationship with the passengers; there was no "privity," and no recovery was allowed. In the spirit of the times, the presiding judge was worried that "if the plaintiff can sue, [then] every passenger, or even any person passing along the road, who was injured by the upsetting of the coach, might bring similar action. Unless we confine the operation of such contracts as this to the parties who entered into them, the most absurd and outrageous consequences, to which I can see no limit, would ensue." [27] The court further held that "this is one of those unfortunate cases in which there certainly has been a *damnum* [damage], but it is a *damnum absque injuria* [damage without violation of a legal right]; it is no doubt a hardship upon the plaintiff to be without a remedy, but by that consideration we ought not to be influenced." [28]

In a climate where the prevailing belief was that each person out for his own greatest gain also produced the greatest gain for society as a whole, as if an invisible hand promoted the greater good, it is no wonder that privity as a judicial doctrine was born. The manufacturer saw himself liable only to the wholesaler, the wholesaler to the retailer, and the retailer to the customer. None of the parties saw obligations to anyone else but those with whom they had contractual relationships, and government laissez-faire and judicial privity decisions confirmed their position.

From 1842 to 1916 a number of inroads were made on the concept of privity, especially in cases involving food, drugs, fire-arms, explosives, other ultrahazardous products, and products involving intimate bodily use. In these cases, the harm done was seen to outweigh the privity concept. And, particularly with respect to bodily-use items, regulations and laws against adulter-ation or improper quality already stretched back to the begin-ning of recorded history. It had long been recognized that the producer or miller of flour, for example, and not solely the vendor, could have a marked influence on its quality [29] and should be held liable accordingly. In many such cases the deci-sions turned aside privity—the producer "had committed fraud" in not labeling his product as adulterated—and found for the plaintiff.

In 1916 came the famous case of the collapsing automobile, *MacPherson v. Buick Motor Company*,[30] in which a defective wheel caused injury. Judge Cardozo, writing for the New York Court of Appeals, held that the manufacturer still was liable, even in the absence of privity, for injuries resulting from the use of a product, whether or not inherently dangerous, if there was evidence of "negligence" in the manufacture or assembly of the product. The judge expressed a view that many had come to regard, especially in the aforementioned food cases, as also re-lating to other types of cases. "We have put aside the notion that the duty to safeguard life and limb, when the consequence of negligence may be foreseen, grows out of contract and nothing else." [31] McKean reviews three cases involving such varied prod-ucts as a sanitary napkin (1928), an inflammable celluloid comb (1930), and a defective bar stool (1953) to show how privity fell in all states and over time as a continuation of the *Mac-Pherson* ruling.

However, an article still had to have the element of intrinsic bodily danger before the courts would consider the abolition of the doctrine of privity.[32] It was not yet "open season" for all types of products, and the changes evolved slowly. Those who were liable included "producers of component parts, assemblers, lessors who rented products to their customers, firms that repaired or reconditioned products, and firms that labeled a product their own even though some other firm actually manufactured the item."[33] Awards for property losses under *MacPherson* were occasionally made, but again, only if the product had posed a significant danger to life and limb.* Coupled with the abolition of privity there also developed an increasing tendency for "plaintiffs' attorneys to name as dependants any and all entities with even a remote connection to the product causing injury or property damage."[35]

Extensions of liability also came about through such doctrines as *res ipsa loquitur:* let the matter speak for itself. The negligence of a bottler for a cockroach in a bottle is self-evident, as it is unlikely anyone would open a container and insert an insect.[36] Further, liability was extended to include guests in a home, master-servant, and other third-party relationships. The maker became liable with respect to anyone who came in contact with the product, not just the purchaser.

Producers' liability also increased with the adoption of the warranty concept. At the outset, let us lay to rest the distinction between guarantee and warranty: there is none. (However, many courts will request that legal briefs mentioning "guarantee" be corrected to read "warranty.") Two types of warranties exist —"express" and "implied"—and these are defined in the Uniform Commercial Code. The Code is a compilation of sales and commercial law which was designated for adoption by each state so that uniform provisions among the states would emerge. The Code was first recommended by the National Conference of Commissioners on Uniform State Laws in 1906 and was finally formulated in 1952 as a replacement for several existing acts, particularly the Uniform Sales Act. The first state to adopt the

* As McKean put it: "Courts have generally refused to make awards for injuries arising from minor hazards, such as a defective high heel or a coffee-can key."[34]

UCC was Pennsylvania, and by 1974 it had been adopted by every state except Louisiana and also by Washington, D.C., and the Virgin Islands. The earlier Uniform Sales Act and Sections 2-313 through 2-318 of the present UCC—which comprise less than two printed pages in all—are the "bibles" of warranty information and reference.

Some people view warranty as an extension of sales law and contracts, while others view it exclusively as a liability device. Its impact is the same regardless of the viewpoint taken.

The first type of warranty is an express warranty, which Anderson and Kumpf define as a part of the basis for the sale; that is, the buyer purchased the goods on the reasonable assumption that they were as stated by the seller." [37] No particular wording is necessary, as an express warranty may be created by any assertion of fact or even by the conduct of the seller. It is immaterial whether the express warranty is made at the time of or after the sale.

An implied warranty is one which is implied by the law rather than made by the seller. The law may read a warranty into a sale even if the seller did not make one expressly. Whereas express warranties form a part of the basis on which a sale is made, implied warranties are interpretations made as a result of a sale.

Express warranties, it should be mentioned, are effective instruments in the defense of liability suits involving property damage. Eginton points out that they do permit a limitation of warranty in property damage situations, in consequential situations,* and in cases involving liability to third parties.[38] However, limitation of liability by a statement such as "liability limited to repair or replacement" has been found to be unconscionable in cases where personal injury is involved. Damages were awarded in a tire-blowout case even though no defect was proven.[39]

Today, every product is considered to have an implied warranty, and all goods sold must be like the sample. It is no

---

* I.e., situations where loss flows from a defective product—for example, loss of photographs due to defective film. The manufacturer limits its warranty to film replacement and not the value of the lost photos.

longer enough for the bulk of such goods to be in reasonable conformity with the sample. The implied warranty poses the bigger of the two liability situations. Section 2-317(1) of the Uniform Commercial Code states: "An implied warranty of merchantability now grows out of every sale where the seller is a merchant, and the UCC defines merchantable to mean that the goods must pass without objection in the trade, have fair average quality fit for ordinary purposes for which the goods are used, be adequately packaged, and fulfill the promises on the container." The UCC also recognizes an implied warranty of fitness for a particular purpose as opposed to the regular purpose of the goods: "Where the seller . . . has reason to know any particular purpose for which the goods are required and that the buyer is relying on the seller's skill or judgment to select or furnish suitable goods, there is . . . an implied warranty that the goods shall be fit for such purpose" (Section 2-315). Under this doctrine, courts have held that the seller should be aware of trade usage—the particular purpose to which goods are put in a particular locality. For example, a screwdriver is used as a pry bar so often that it should be manufactured to withstand this use or to fail in a non-injurious manner (bend rather than snapping off with flying pieces).

An implied warranty can be nullified if the purchaser refuses to inspect the product or fails to detect defects that an adequate inspection should have revealed.[40] A seller can also sell an item "as is," eliminating all implied warranties, if he makes it clear that he is doing so.

Advertising directly to consumers can create warranties to them, as the Ford Motor Company found out when it advertised "shatterproof" windshields—which did shatter when hit by a rock.[41] Manufacturers must, in the face of the difficulties posed by implied warranties, carefully word their express warranties and protect themselves against at least property damage and "remote consequences" claims. Insurance carriers are very alert to the dangers of unlimited property claims. Commercial losses can be enormous when, for example, a defective process monitor fails to signal an overheat condition and an entire refinery blows up.

The "remote consequences" may be loss of profits and contracts over several years.

In 1960, *Henningsen v. Bloomfield Motors, Inc.*[42] signaled the end of privity as an effective defense regardless of the product. A Mrs. Henningsen, driving a car purchased by her husband, was injured when the car suddenly veered and ran into a wall. The court held both the manufacturer (Chrysler) and the dealer liable under the implied warranty. The court saw "no rational doctrinal basis for differentiating between a fly in a bottle of beverage and a defective automobile." [43]

At about the same time, a movement was developing to hold producers and merchants to strict liability under tort. A tort is a civil wrong in which sanctions are imposed to make the injured part whole again—most often monetary payments.

Strict liability under tort means a producer, or anyone else in the stream of commerce who may have caused a defect, is held liable because a wrong was done or a duty neglected. The plaintiff in a suit must prove that a defect existed in the product; he does not have to prove that either negligence or a contract existed for him to hold the producer liable.

When privity was "downed" under *Henningsen,* the movement toward strict liability was accelerated. *Goldberg v. Kollsman Instrument Corp. et al.*[44] illustrates how the courts searched for a just compromise among conflicting interests while imposing strict liability in tort. A defective altimeter allegedly caused an aircraft crash, and the estate of a deceased passenger sued the airline, the altimeter manufacturer, and the aircraft manufacturer. The New York Court of Appeals rested its decision on the law of tort, holding against the aircraft manufacturer while freeing the altimeter firm because the "airplane manufacturer's liability [legal responsibility backed up by its recognized considerable resources] provided sufficient protection to the passengers." [45] Further extending this decision, many courts hold that the strict-liability doctrine is not applicable to a component supplier who knows his component will be assembled by the purchaser into a completed part. But here too there are exceptions, as we will discuss later.

Other cases involved defective designs in a power tool, which injured the user by hurling a piece of wood through the air, and a truck whose improper weight distribution caused it to "gallop" and eventually overturn.[46] In the latter case, the court went out of its way to say that the law drew a distinction between tort recovery for physical injuries and warranty recovery for economic loss, and refused recovery of economic damages under tort.

These types of cases yielded confusing decisions until the American Law Institute attacked the problem by issuing its *Restatement of the Law of Torts* in 1965. The Institute, which was founded in 1923, has the objective of presenting an orderly statement of the general common law of the United States. The Institute includes in the term "general common law" not only common law as previously defined but also case law and law which has grown from the courts' application of statutes that have been in force for many years.[47] The restatements promulgated by the Institute represent the expert opinion and expression of the law by the legal profession. They are designed to preempt the need for rigid legislation by "cutting through" irreconcilable case decisions and complications of common law. Many courts accept the Institute's restatements as the prima facie correct statements of the general law of the United States.

The first tort restatement work was issued in 1934, but it was the 1965 volume which contained a section (402A) that has become almost the standard reference on product liability. Titled "Special Liability of Seller of Product for Physical Harm to User or Consumer," the section consists of two one-sentence paragraphs with two qualifying sentences each.[48] The first paragraph says that one who sells a product in a defective condition that is unreasonably dangerous to a consumer or his property is subject to liability for physical harm. There are two qualifications: The seller must be in the business of selling such a product, and the product must have reached the user without substantial change in the condition in which it was sold. The second paragraph says the rule applies even if the seller exercised all possible care in preparation and sale of the product and even if there has not been any contractual relationship of any kind between consumer and seller. The word "seller" includes manufacturer, wholesaler, retailer, distributor, and even restaurant operator.

The justification for strict liability has been that the seller who markets a product has assumed a special responsibility toward any member of the consuming public who may be injured by it. The burden of accidental injuries caused by products should be placed upon those who market them and be treated as a cost of production, for which liability insurance can be obtained.[49]

Note that while the rule extends to any product sold in the condition, or substantially the same condition, in which it is expected to reach the ultimate user (such as stoves, chairs, or tires), the rule leaves hanging the question of items that are processed or assembled. Courts have held that even if a product undergoes further processing or is serviced before delivery, liability may still rest with a manufacturer who sold it at a prior stage, particularly if the fault should have been discovered or prevented at that stage. The auto manufacturer is responsible, for example, for a defective steering gear, as is a coffee grower even if someone else roasts his poisoned beans.

As noted above, the Institute's rule applies to any person engaged in the business of selling products for use or consumption. It exempts a casual seller who is not in business but is making only an incidental sale between friends or a sale on a one-time basis. The product must be proved to have been defective when it left the hands of the seller, with the burden of proof on the injured plaintiff. The seller is *not* liable if he delivers the product in a safe condition and the user subsequently abuses or misuses the product and renders it unsafe. Misuse and abuse, or "contributory negligence," refers to instances where the plaintiff brought his injuries upon himself. The claim of contributory negligence is a powerful defense tool when the plaintiff seeks to hold the manufacturer strictly liable in tort. The manufacturer, in effect, says that the defect was generated or turned into an accident situation by the plaintiff. A defendant who can prove that contributory negligence on the part of the plaintiff was the only way an accident could have taken place, or that the plaintiff's negligence contributed to the injury, defeats the plaintiff's claim.

Ordinarily this defeat is total—the plaintiff gets nothing even if the defendant was more negligent than he. However, a number of states have statutes calling for comparison of the negligence of defendant and plaintiff. Plaintiff's negligence does not bar recovery but merely reduces the amount in proportion to the degree or extent of his own negligence. (This is the doctrine of comparative negligence.)

The term "unreasonably dangerous," as used in Section 402A, has been interpreted to mean dangerous to an extent beyond that contemplated by the ordinary consumer with ordinary knowledge. A parent, for example, cannot sue the candy company when his or her child becomes ill from consuming a dozen candy bars. However, the seller is expected to warn the consumer when there is reason to believe that a consumer with ordinary knowledge would not know about certain ingredients in the product or their harmful effects. In cases where a drug with harmful side effects must be administered, the product is considered to be *not* unreasonably dangerous if its purpose is to combat a more serious illness, and the physician and patient are so advised (warned).

In addition to breach of warranty and strict liability in tort, the plaintiff's attorney can charge negligence on the part of all those who put the product into the stream of commerce. Simply put, negligence means:

You did something you should not have done,
or
You failed to do something you should have done.

It is the manufacturer's duty to design, construct, test, inspect, and warn the user so that (1) the product is safe for all intended and foreseeable uses; (2) if it fails, it will fail in a noninjurious manner; and (3) the user is informed of all precautions and risks inherent in its use. Most court fights in this area of the law hinge on the words "intended" and "foreseeable." A carpenter's hammer is not intended as a substitute for a sledgehammer, but use against a wide variety of materials (not just nails and wood) is foreseeable. It should not chip and cause injury.

To prove that he was not negligent, the manufacturer must demonstrate, as applicable:

1. That he took all precautions in design, construction, etc., commensurate with the state of the art when the product was built.
2. That none of the seven types of plaintiff allegations (p. 4) apply to this case.
3. That he complied with all product safety statutes, complied with administrative law,* and in particular was in full conformance with the custom, practice, and standards of the industry.

When a product carries the insignia of a national standards-making organization, compliance with the standard can be used before a jury to show full conformance with industry custom and practice. Plaintiff attorneys attack this, saying that "industry makes the custom and practice whence come the standards, and the latter are no defense." If the standards have been used as a cheap way of incorporating the lowest common denominator of industry practices, instead of meaningful quality and care, the standard is effectively destroyed in court and used to embarrass the defense. However, meaningful standards do impress juries. We will return to negligence in later chapters. It is important because plaintiff attorneys find it to be a powerful charge easily explained to a jury and because it permits recovery not only for injury but for economic damages as well.

Finally, we call your attention here (and will do so again in later chapters) to a point that continuously confounds business-men. The statute of limitations, the time limit within which a suit may be brought, starts from the day of the accident or the day of realization that injury has been sustained (if it occurred insidiously over a long period of time) and not from the day the product was built, if it can be proved a defect existed from the day it left the seller's hands. Legislatures are moving, gradually, to impose statutes of limitations on the work of professional people from the day their work is completed or a structure erected, but nothing comparable appears to be in the works for products. Still, it should be kept in mind that the law is an evolving instrument.

---

* I.e., rules and regulations set up by a governing body which have the force of law until challenged in court.

Philo says: "The law is not what the courts said the last time—the law is what the courts will say in your case." [50]

To close this discussion of the law, we should mention the increasing number of "long-arm statutes" that legislatures are enacting. Such a statute subjects a manufacturer to the jurisdiction of a state solely on the basis of a tort committed within that state. A firm's product causing an injury in that state can result in a lawsuit there, even if the firm did no business there and the product was simply carried in. In many states, the same effect has been achieved by judicial decisions.

Defenses against foreign suits will be discussed in Chapter 5.

INSURANCE

Product liability insurance is a contract with an underwriter or internal mechanism set up to pay damages for bodily injury or destruction of property arising out of the products produced or sold by the insured. Hedges, restrictions, and additions to the above simplified definition are covered in Chapter 5. Our key point here is that insurance is for the fortuitous event and should not apply—indeed, may not apply—in cases where the injury could have been foreseen (and prevented or warned against) by the manufacturer.

As we mentioned earlier, product liability insurers are putting more and more limitations on their coverage of property damages and remote-consequences damages. They are demanding strict accountability in performance from their insureds before they cover claims under warranty, strict liability, and negligence. They do not want carelessness on the factory floor to be translated into higher claims from product users.

The decade of the 1970s is one of upheaval in the insurance field, and many manufacturers are beginning to find that making quick, unresearched decisions—and using a traditional general insurance broker when purchasing liability protection—is not the wisest course to follow. It may even be dangerous, if the result is simply maintenance of a many-years-old status quo. Insurance, like the law, is evolving and constantly changing.

Initially, in the World War I years, product liability insurance covered only foreign substances in products meant for human consumption. The courts still, by and large, shielded manufacturers of other types of products against liability for their negligence. However, as the law changed, more and more products, of an ever increasing complexity, were brought under coverage. Insurance firms took greater and greater financial beatings as damage awards and case volume soared. Legal costs rose steeply.

In response to this, in October 1966 the National Bureau of Casualty Underwriters made sweeping changes in the contract provisions of the standard general liability policy used by its insureds.[51] The changes, ostensibly made to clarify the scope of coverage, excluded products (or completed operations) if they caused harm due to the product's failure to perform as intended if the failure was due to: (1) mistake or deficiency in design; (2) mistake in formula, plan, or specification; or (3) mistake in advertising or printed instructions. Actual malfunction of the product or work was still covered; if it hadn't been, the insurance would have served no function.

It turned out that the changes were made because of claim volume and high damage awards suffered by underwriters. They not only changed their forms, adding new exclusions, but increased their rates and, as Howell described it, placed on a taboo list "the manufacturer of virtually every mechanical or electrical product made." [52] Class actions were effectively eliminated as a threat to most firms by a Supreme Court finding that in order to mount such a suit the plaintiffs had to notify each and every member of the proposed class and obtain his or her consent.[53] The plaintiffs could no longer simply name thousands of "John Does," sue in their behalf, and then try to distribute winnings (after the deduction of large legal fees) to all those who afterwards applied for consideration in the case.

A lack of insurance can kill off new products, especially in the medical field, and can severely curtail existing services. The risks will simply not be deemed worth the potential profits. Banks have refused to capitalize certain product development work where it was impossible to obtain the stipulated product liability insurance. The insurance industry, afraid of risky new products manufactured by untested firms, has contributed to the increasing industrial concentration that many people see as the antithesis of our free enterprise system. Some suggestions and answers for existing firms are offered in Chapter 5, but there are no broad-based solutions in sight. The problem of having a new product (or even a new industry) die before its birth because the unavailability of liability coverage choked off capitalization is still very much with us.

WHAT THIS BOOK SHOULD DO FOR YOU

As noted in the preface, this book offers information that will help you learn from the first experience or avoid it altogether. If you are hit with a suit, you will know what to expect: You will learn just how a claim against a company is instituted and supported, especially the concepts that may be used in attacking a product. You will learn how your defense team should function and some of the things to avoid in a trial situation. You will examine the question of insurance coverage—whether your insurance gives you a sufficient financial buffer against lawsuits or whether it contains loopholes that leave you without protection. You will be offered some suggestions for a complete approach to a product liability prevention program, some words on keeping current, and some prognostications for the future.

If you have not become convinced that product liability is a problem worthy of serious attention, we feel you will most certainly acknowledge it after completing this book. You will see the possibility of your having to join with others in defending against a suit, even if you did nothing wrong. You will see that you may be asked to spread the cost of injury by absorbing damages and passing them on in price increases. You will see how old products can come back to haunt you, and how what you said or didn't say in selling your product can be used against you. And if you did not carefully insure yourself, you will pay the bill.

REFERENCES

1. See Peter Vanderwicken, "Toward the Socialization of Injury," *Fortune* (November 1971), pp. 161–181.
2. For example, *Product Liability Reporter* (New York: Commerce Clearing House), a regular publication listing judgments and regulatory actions related to product liability; Louis R. Frumer and Melvin I. Friedman, *Products Liability* (New York: Matthew Bender, 1971), a compendium of regularly updated cases; and the *Insurance Law Journal.*
3. "Accident Victims Recover Less Than One-Half Their Losses," *The New York Times,* April 29, 1970, p. 1.
4. Nicholas M. Stiglich, "Manufacturer's Product Liability," master's thesis, Polytechnic Institute of Brooklyn, June 1965.
5. For a complete analysis of the obsolescence of professional personnel, see H. G. Kaufman, *Obsolescence and Professional Career Development* (New York: AMACOM, 1974).
6. See the outstanding *Fortune* series on "Embattled Consumer Products," in the January 1972 through June 1972 issues. See also "The Pressure Is On for Safer Products," *Business Week* (July 4, 1970), p. 36.
7. See *Final Report, National Commission on Product Safety* (Washington, D.C.: U.S. Government Printing Office, 1970).
8. See Joel Dean, *Managerial Economics* (Englewood Cliffs, N.J.: Prentice-Hall, 1951), Chapter 4.
9. Ibid.
10. *Quality Progress* (January 1970), p. 5.
11. "The Pressure Is On for Safer Products," op. cit.
12. Franz S. F. Lerner, "Quality Control in Pre-Industrial Times," *Quality Progress* (June 1970), p. 22.
13. Ibid., p. 23.
14. Ibid.
15. Ibid., p. 24.
16. Ibid.
17. Adam Smith, *The Wealth of Nations* (New York: The Modern Library, 1937), p. 24. Originally published 1776.
18. Ibid., p. 25.
19. Lerner, op. cit., p. 25.
20. Ronald A. Anderson and Walter A. Kumpf, *Business Law,* 9th ed./Uniform Commercial Code (Cincinnati: South-Western Publishing Company, 1973), p. 1.

21. Ibid., p. 2.
22. Ibid.
23. Ibid.
24. Roland N. McKean, "Products Liability: Trends and Implications," *University of Chicago Law Review*, Vol. 38, No. 1 (Fall 1970), p. 6.
25. 152 Eng. Rep. 402 (Ex. 1842).
26. Smith, op. cit., p. 423.
27. 152 Eng. Rep. at 405.
28. Ibid.
29. King John of England's 1202 Food Law, the Assize of Bread; the 1784 Massachusetts General Food Law; and the 1824 Flour Inspection Act of Alexandria, Virginia.
30. 217 N.Y., 382 III N.E., 1050 (1916).
31. MacPherson v. Buick Motor Company, op. cit. (note 30).
32. McKean, op. cit., p. 10.
33. Ibid.
34. Ibid.
35. Warren W. Eginton, "Manufacturers Legal Responsibility for Quality of Purchased Supplies," *Proceedings, PLP70*, Product Liability Prevention Conference, August 26–28, 1970, p. 161.
36. Escola v. Coca-Cola Bottling Co., 24 Cal. 2d 453, 150 P. 2d 436 (1944).
37. Anderson and Kumpf, op. cit., p. 511.
38. Eginton, op. cit., p. 163.
39. Collins v. Uniroyal, Inc. (New Jersey), A7113 (June 1973): aff'd. P. 7114 (February 1974).
40. Collum v. Pope & Talbot, 135 Cal. App. 2d 784, 288 P. 2d 75 (1955). Cited in McKean, op. cit., p. 13.
41. 168 Wash. 456, 12 P. 2d 409 (1932).
42. 32 N.J. 358, 161 A. 2d 69 (1960).
43. Ibid.
44. 12 N.Y. 2d 432, 191 N.E. 2d 81, 240 N.Y.S. 2d 592 (1963).
45. McKean, op. cit., p. 15.
46. Greenman v. Yuba Power Products Inc., 59 Cal. 2d 57, 377 P. 2d 897, 27 Cal. Rptr. 697 (1963); and Seely v. White Motor Co., 63 Cal. 2d 9, 403 P. 2d 145, 45 Cal. Rptr. 17 (1965).
47. American Law Institute, *Torts* (St. Paul, Minn.: American Law Institute Publishers, 1938), Introduction.
48. American Law Institute, *Restatement (Second) of the Law:*

Torts (St. Paul, Minn.: American Law Institute Publishers, 1965), Chapter 14, Section 402A, commentary.

49. Ibid.

50. Harry M. Philo, attorney, makes this point in his public lectures and in Dean A. Robb, Harry M. Philo, and Richard M. Goodman, *Lawyers Desk Reference* (Rochester, N.Y.: Lawyers Cooperative Publishing Company, 1971), p. vi.

51. *Products Liability and Reliability: Some Management Considerations* (Washington, D.C.: Machinery and Allied Products Institute, 1967), pp. 131–168. Cited in Edward B. Howell, "The Counterproductivity of Product and Professional Liability Claims," *Consulting Engineer* (September 1971), p. 70.

52. Howell, op. cit., p. 70.

53. "High Court Curbs Suits on Behalf of Large Groups," *The New York Times*, May 29, 1974, p. 1.

2

THE PLAINTIFF
BUILDS
HIS CASE

A company's success in defending against a product liability
suit depends on three main factors: (1) the nature of the accident—who was injured or what was damaged; (2) the legal
expertise of the attorney seeking damages; and (3) the competency of the experts who examine the product and supply the
technical testimony.

In this chapter we will examine these factors by sequentially
tracing the plaintiff's side of a case from well before the institution of a suit through the completion of all the pretrial work.
In our view, the technical person who examines the product that
allegedly caused the injury or damage is a key person in achiev-
ing success for the plaintiff attorney: His role will be extensively
analyzed in unfolding the case procedure. Coverage of the plaintiff's actions will be counterpointed, from time to time, with items
pertaining to company policies and operations, though these will
be more fully detailed in Chapter 3.

We include this chapter for the managerial reader because
a successful defense starts with a complete understanding of the
attacker's origins and motivations, and of the adversary procedures used in the legal system of the United States.

ACCIDENTS

The causes and effects of product-related accidents are adequately documented by the National Safety Council and various government agencies. For our purposes it is sufficient to note that in a commercial environment, product failure can cause any combination of personal injury, property damage, and business interruption. In the home, personal injury usually overshadows consideration of the property damage.

Most product failures do not result in significant damages, and the people involved simply absorb the physical or financial damage as part of the hazards of daily life. Nuisance claims of the sort that have become notorious in the automobile negligence field are highly unlikely, for two reasons:

1. Product liability litigation is extremely expensive to the plaintiff. He or she has to bankroll a case that will involve an expert to examine the product (several hundred to a thousand dollars); time spent by the attorney in obtaining depositions, i.e., sworn records of pretrial questioning of all possible defendants (up to hundreds of dollars); and attorney travel expenses to the plant, wholesaler, and retailer (again, hundreds of dollars). While many attorneys will pay these expenses out of "disbursement" accounts instead of immediately dunning the clients for them, it is the client who must pay whether the case is won or lost because it is against the law for an attorney to foster litigation by subsidizing it—a practice called champerty.

2. "Nuisance" product liability cases are difficult to win. They may be contrasted with automobile accident cases, in which the opposing attorneys will argue over the degree of negligence displayed in one or two acts of the opposing parties. These cases are tried by many attorneys without depositions at minimal expense and settled directly between opposition parties without going to trial (or even expecting to). In product liability suits, however, the ramifications of proved negligence by a corporation are enormous, and it will resist suit. While the bulk of these cases are settled before trial, the plaintiff attorney must prepare his case as if he will fight to the highest appeals court, because

FIGURE 1. Electric range heating element.

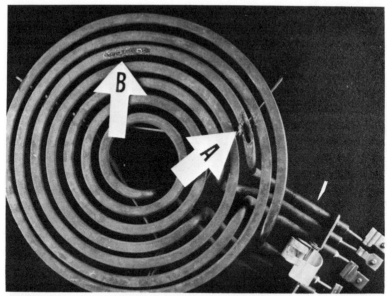

(a) Points of deterioration at A and B

(b) Closeup of point A damage

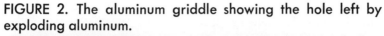

FIGURE 2. The aluminum griddle showing the hole left by exploding aluminum.

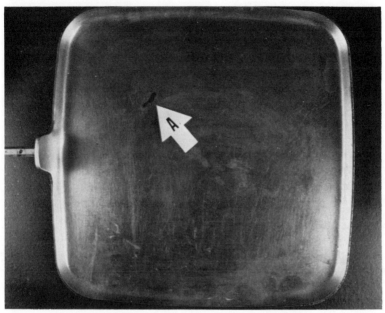

if he shows that he has not so prepared himself, his ability to settle the case at a satisfactory level goes to zero.

When an injured party first communicates with a firm, it will often be as an inquiry in the most innocent fashion: "What happened to our flower bed? It does not seem to respond properly to your fertilizer treatment," masking a disaster in which a large commercial flower bed was chemically burned out. Or, the communication may be a simple complaint that something went wrong and "could you please rectify the damage."

Figure 1 illustrates an electric range heating element that had deteriorated at point B and became totally damaged at point A. The element exploded at point A, melted the griddle shown in Figure 2, and showered a homemaker and her kitchen with BB-sized pellets of molten aluminum. (Figure 3 shows a closeup of the hole left in the griddle.) She had, fortunately, just turned

FIGURE 3. Closeup of hole left by exploding aluminum (approximately 1.5 times actual size).

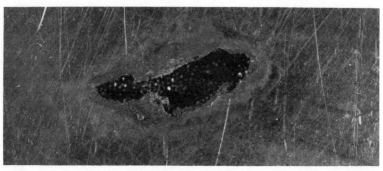

away from the stove when the failure occurred: Her hair and housedress were singed instead of her face. This woman's letter to the range manufacturer (one of our nation's giant multi-product firms) cited these damages plus a ruined countertop and psychic trauma. She asked for a new burner element and $157 for all other damages, consisting of reimbursement for the countertop, a haircut, a new housedress, some paint work, and so on.

Which brings us to the response people get when they complain to the manufacturer or his dealers—and the reasons why many suits which should have been obviated are mounted and severely prosecuted.

In the flower bed case, two things happened as a matter of course: An overdue notice was sent on the bill, and a semi-interested salesman bucked the letter "to the boys at headquarters." The customer received a bill for a product that had wreaked havoc on his business and a loud silence regarding his complaint. Constant inquiries revealed that his complaint was being bucked from department to department, with the firm's final decision being "to replace the unused portion of fertilizer with a different product." Bills and increasing credit department pressures arrived regularly.

The customer retained an attorney. He sought and won damages for loss of the field, refund of the full cost of the fertilizer, damages for future business losses, and a host of additional consequential damages.

The immediate response of the range element manufacturer was to service the range by replacing the element and presenting a bill. The homemaker refused to pay and sent letters to the firm asking again for the small reimbursement for damages and cancellation of the service bill. Eventually, letters were sent to everyone from the corporate president down to the local service manager. Months passed with no response to the letters but with regular overdue notices on the bill. A final letter sent to the firm by the woman's husband contained the implicit threat that an attorney would be retained and damages sought for "loss of wife's services," "psychic trauma," and a host of additional items. Finally a check arrived—along with a release form for the customer to sign and another overdue notice for the service bill. It took several more calls to get the bill canceled.

Moral: Often the plaintiff's case can be nipped in the bud by common-sense decency and a relaxation of billing procedures until the product has rendered satisfaction.

THE PLAINTIFF ATTORNEY

The client who considers instituting a suit little realizes that the process can run five years or more, will put in his employ attorneys, researchers, and engineers, and will require a substantial financial investment on his part. The attorney will listen to the client's story and immediately evaluate whether or not there is a case: Has there been sufficient personal, physical, or business injury or combination thereof?

The attorney should also ask: What are the expectations, characteristics, and requirements of the plaintiff?

Some plaintiffs follow a self-defeating course. There is the plaintiff who has unduly high expectations for an award and makes unrealistic demands on his or her attorney. It is not an uncommon occurrence for such a client to become disenchanted with the best efforts of his counsel, to disobey instructions at crucial times, and to contribute to the loss of a reasonable case.

Some clients are large businesses that can obviously afford a large case, and therefore seem formidable at first. However, top management often loses interest in its own cause under the press of more urgent matters, or when officers of the firm find themselves losing time with interrogations, depositions, court appearances, and what seems to be an endless series of conferences with their attorney. What started as a suit with "blood in the eye" may peter out as a totally insignificant settlement. (To this end, some defendants will deliberately stretch a case out for the longest time possible, making it virtually automatic to appeal to a higher court no matter what the level of loss at the first trial.) Some suits with potentially high awards due to consequential damages will be aborted by the plaintiffs themselves because revealing to the court the proof necessary to justify the damage award would reveal too much proprietary information.

So, even when there is sufficient evidence of injury, certain characteristics of the plaintiff may make the case a difficult one for the plaintiff attorney. Especially on a contingency fee basis, the attorney must have hopes of recovering a reasonable amount of money on a case. Is there a specific product and a worthwhile defendant? If the exact cause is part of an amorphous sequence of events, and/or a defendant is a marginal uninsured little business, hopes of recovery of substantial monetary compensation are usually small enough to cause the most prominent attorneys in the liability field to turn the case away.

The attorney must also examine the jurisdiction and the law that will most likely apply to the case. On the subject of jurisdiction, we have already mentioned the effects of long-arm statutes: Even if a product was made, sold, and distributed only for use in a remote state, suit could conceivably be brought in the jurisdiction familiar to the attorney. This obviously aids his efficiency in prosecuting the suit and, later, in collecting damages. There are also many instances where a local retailer or small manufacturer is the sole target even though strict liability or negligence could be properly alleged to a remote supplier—with the potential for a much larger recovery.

As to the law that best applies to the case, we have mentioned warranty, strict liability in tort, and negligence. These are the main charges around which the plaintiff attorney can structure a case. However, he or she can flesh them out with gleanings from the *Lawyers Desk Reference* (*LDR*),[1] which provides a checklist of 20 different legal theories of liability from virtually every aspect of the law which can be stretched to apply to product liability cases. If the plaintiff attorney puts in a little effort, the chance of losing an opportunity for recovery due to overlooking a legal concept is reduced to nil.* The checklist also gives fourteen legal theories of defense against tort claims. So the plaintiff attorney cannot be surprised by the defendant's raising an issue that he or she is unable to effectively cover in legal briefs and future arguments in court. As in a chess game, all the pieces are on the board for both sides to see. The rules and boundaries are clearly marked; it's only the sequence of moves that yields the outcome.

Next we turn to the entire question of the evidence in the case—with the number one item, of course, being the product which caused or is alleged to have caused the accident.

After the specific product has been identified, the plaintiff attorney will exert every effort to obtain physical control of it. It becomes the charge of the attorney and the attorney's engineer to pinpoint the role of the item in the accident and to identify some specific negligence on the part of those who put it into the stream of commerce. For accidents occurring in home settings, the injured party usually owns the item. He or she turns it over to the attorney or stores it under lock and key. In industrial settings, access to the culprit product (a machine on an assembly line, for example) is gained through the owner's cooperation or is forced by means of a court order.

In cases where the injury or damage has been caused over a long period of time (in insurance terms "caused by an occurrence") rather than by a single cataclysmic event, the evidence is much harder to pinpoint. Extensive medical tests may be necessary to show which gas in the blood caused a toxic reaction,

---

* Business would do well to consider the damning implications of the philosophy that *LDR* preaches an attorney should hold as he attacks the defendant: They knew nothing, cared nothing, and did nothing about safety.[2]

and this information tells the investigator what to look for in the factory or other location. A fertilizer which does not fertilize may have as disastrous an economic effect on a grower as one which burns out the bed, but tracing it as the source of the damage is much more difficult. Gases, noise, shock, and vibration are being increasingly recognized as great dangers because of cumulative effects on the body even though short exposures are considered harmless. Collecting the evidence in such cases requires an enormous amount of ingenuity and the services of a professional engineer.

The attorney will call in an engineer to render a preliminary technical opinion in some cases, a full verbal opinion in others, or a full written report in still others. A preliminary opinion is used when the aggrieved party's story is incomplete and the attorney wants the engineer to answer the question: Could the accident have taken place as the client alleges? Perhaps there was a rationalization in the person's mind, or some personal fault that is being concealed in the client's story. Or perhaps shock and pain of personal injury have led to the reconstruction of an impossible situation. If the client, confronted with the engineer's opinion, cannot refresh his memory or resolve inconsistencies, the attorney may refuse to handle the case further. This "screening" process never stops, as the attorney, client, and engineer continuously resolve every contradiction that reveals itself throughout the development of the suit and the trial. The corollary is self-evident: The corporate manager who expects a claimant's case to be blown apart as soon as his own engineers go over it will generally be disappointed. The screening process usually weeds out such cases.

The choice between a full verbal report and a full written report is usually made by the attorney, who directs the engineer accordingly. Avoidance of a written report is a trial-preparation technique. In some states, the defense can legally order the engineer to make available his entire file for their examination. Reports found in it are then dissected word for word. How this works may be illustrated by a case involving a riding lawn mower. The engineer's report was ordered entered in evidence when he testified that the mower's brakes did not hold sufficiently to stop the mower safely. Cross-examination by the defense attorney focused on this report and took into account that the engineer had repeatedly written the words "wheels sliding" in describing the stopping action of the mower with the brakes engaged. The defense attorney pointedly called attention to the fact that the tendency of wheels to slide is a function of the ground they are traversing and claimed that the very words proved the brake system was strong enough to lock the wheels. The witness made a poor showing of himself as he lamely maintained that he meant wheels *rolling* over the ground.

An additional problem with the written report is the fact that written words tend to lock the engineer into a possible premature conclusion. For example, a preliminary investigation into a tire failure yielded no results, and this was reported as part of a continuing investigation by the engineer. Later, depositions pointed to a more specific problem, and a detailed, focused investigation resulted in a report charging the tire company with negligence in construction. Both reports were in a file that the defendant forced the engineer to place in evidence at the trial. The result of the contradiction between the two reports, at the trial, was that the engineer's credibility was seriously impeached before the jury. He had to spend more time explaining why he had changed his opinions and what had influenced his opinions than he spent discussing the tire. So most attorneys will ask for a full written report only when the product and the causes of the problem are complex and the report is needed for extended study.

Just what does an engineer do for his client, and how does he enter into the litigation process? Most important is his supposed professional objectivity. He may be retained by the plaintiff attorney and paid his fee by the plaintiff, but his report and testimony are expected to be without bias; only the facts should influence his conclusions and opinions. While the existing fee relationship casts some doubt on the degree of neutrality he brings to the case, it is considered to be more enlightening in the cause of justice, and closer to the whole truth, to retain an independent professional engineer than to use an engineer who has some connection with either side.

It might be mentioned in passing that it is not unusual for attorneys for the defendant to also retain independent professional engineers, even though the defendant firm could tap its own virtually unlimited reserves of engineering talent. This calling in of outside people often irks the engineering manager of the defendant firm, who views the consultant as a less knowledgeable addition to the case than one of the insiders who has worked on the device since its inception. But the appearance of objectivity is extremely important for defendant as well as plaintiff, and it is up to the defense team, engineering manager included, to close the consultant's knowledge gaps.

It should also be mentioned that this procedure of using an outside expert is not without a fair degree of corruption possibilities. When the plaintiff attorney and the engineering consultant first meet to discuss the case, the attorney will listen intently for an opinion he wants to hear no matter how cautiously voiced. If he doesn't hear it or gets no response to some choice ideas he "tosses out," he may thank the engineer politely, pay the fee (usually small or nonexistent, as the engineer wants to be called again), and call someone else from his long list of available free-lance "experts," college professors, people in the industry, and people recommended by other attorneys. Engineers who are no strangers to the courtroom are ultra-quick to pick up the rightfulness of the potential client's case, and some attorneys are all too willing to plant ideas contrary to the engineer's expressed opinion. One preventive against corruption, however, is the fact that these contrary opinions sometimes emerge as doubts (or worse) under skillful cross-examination. This is embarrassing, to say the least, to the attorney who retained the engineer.

The first stage in the engineer's investigation is to gather information. He or she reads all written material the attorney has about the case—usually some testimony by the injured party alleging what happened and the events leading up to the incident. Then the engineer gathers any available data from commercial literature, scholarly journals of engineering societies, or government bulletins about the failure characteristics of the product and its component materials. Industry codes and safety standards that were effective as of the date of manufacture of the product will be examined. Consumer protection agencies on the federal, state, and local levels will be tapped for information about problems with specific consumer goods. Government occupational health and safety agencies and the National Safety Council provide further information. A whole array of organizations (including competing firms, as mentioned in Chapter 1) can provide a wealth of information about safety characteristics and features for different classes of products. For example, assume product A caused an injury because its blades lacked a guard. If product B has a guard for its blades and it was designed, built, and marketed at the same time as product A, the company cannot claim a guard "was beyond the state of the art" and exposure to injury was part of the user's assumed risk. Similarly, certain firms use cheaper components with fewer positive locking features on one part of the product line and more positive (read "safer") items on the more expensive parts of the product line. The contrast can be used in court to show that the firm compromised safety to a terribly disproportionate degree in order to save dollars.

Corporate managers should not be shy about turning regularly to the consultant's sources of information, including *LDR*, to widen their thinking and perceptions beyond the four walls of the firm. They should keep in touch with all the groups mentioned, have their people keep up to date on the state of the art through scholarly journals, and above all remain aware of safety improvements in the industry. More specifics about the foregoing are reserved for a later chapter, as is the problem of cost versus safety reductions.

THE ENGINEER'S EXAMINATION OF THE PRODUCT

To cover the full details of how an accident investigation determines causality and attending negligence would go beyond the scope of this book; it would entail exploring numerous engineering disciplines, from metallurgy to human factors engineering.[3] What is important here is how the engineer ties his work to the eventual court trial for which he must, at all times, be prepared. He conducts his investigation in the framework of two legal concepts—negligence and *res ipsa loquitur*. These concepts are also excellent bases from which (on the other side of the fence) the alert manager can cast a critical eye on his firm's products.

The engineer attempts to show that the defendant created a "hazard" and an undue "risk" to the user. Philo gives a very succinct definition of hazard which we can apply here. He says a hazard is a condition or changing set of circumstances that presents an injury potential.[4] The degeneration in the electric range heating element shown in Figure 1 was an example of a condition. Moving jaws of a power press are a changing set of circumstances. Risk, which we will cover more completely in Chapter 5, is the probability of injury. Philo points out that risk is based on two factors: exposure and proximity.[5] The homemaker using the defective heating element of her stove had less exposure in preparing three meals a day than would a restaurant short order cook. Proximity is, of course, how close one is to the hazard. If the heating element had been under a truly shatter-proof heat-conducting glass, its explosion would have been physically remote from the griddle and the shower of aluminum pellets would not have resulted.

Some hazards can be termed "negligible" or "safe" because malfunctions will not result in injury or damage. When an engineer is called in on a case, he cannot overlook that this may indeed be true of the product at hand, even if it is alleged to have caused an accident. He must keep an open mind. There is risk inherent in the use of virtually any product or service—including, for example, a common table knife. Many risks are "open and notorious," such as the fact that a meat grinder can do serious damage to fingers caught in it. People frequently assume some risk when using a product, but a manufacturer's negligence may raise the combination of hazard and risk to an unacceptable level.

The key points to be considered by the engineer are: (1) Could reasonable prevention or prudent care have eliminated the exposure or proximity? (2) Could the risk have been recognized by the user? In the case of the defective heating element, the risk in using the element as it degenerated at points A and B could not have been recognized by the ordinary homemaker, as it continued to heat up and render normal service until the accident.

Negligence

To prove negligence, the engineer must trace accident causality to some negligent act that affected the product as it moved from conception to the point of delivery to the customer. The manufacturer of the product is usually the primary target in the chain for the simple reason that he is usually the richest link; it is felt that he should have foreseen what would happen as his product moved from his doors to the customer, and he should have taken precautions accordingly. Barring an outright, obvious act of negligence on the part of the distributor or retailer, the manufacturer will wind up taking the brunt of any damage suit. Also, all other defendants in the suit are most happy to shift blame to the manufacturer.

The consultant, therefore, will look for signs of manufacturer negligence in any of the following five areas:

Design
Construction (materials and/or workmanship)
Inspection
Testing
Warning (labeling and/or user directions)

We have defined negligence as a party doing something he should not have done or not doing something he should have done. The engineer seeks to demonstrate that some action or lack of action within one or more of the five areas created a situation which led to someone suffering a physical or financial loss.

Design. Design cases are usually the ones most hard fought by manufacturers, because "the plaintiff is not just attacking the single specific product that caused his injuries. He is, in effect, claiming that any product made by the defendant designed in the same way is defective." [6] As Frumer and Friedman put it, the manufacturer must "exercise ordinary care in designing his product so that it is reasonably safe for the purposes for which it is intended." [7] For many products, this "ordinary care" is strictly defined by national standards and industry custom. However, as mentioned before, the plaintiff can and often does attack these as "industry whitewash" to protect designs at the lowest common denominator of industry agreement.* In other words, if standards exist and the product meets the standards, the plaintiff attacks the standards. If there are standards and the product fails in any way to meet the standards, then the product is attacked for "not even meeting accepted industry practice."

Sometimes foreign standards provide a good foundation for proving that a safety device was within the state of the art at the time the product was built. Attorneys will examine European, Russian, and Japanese standards, many of which have been far more strict in demanding the incorporation of safety devices than comparable American standards. The United Kingdom, Germany, the Netherlands, and Sweden will on occasion hold products to tighter electrical safety parameters, demand more redundant safety features, or demand a more fail-safe operation than even the strictest U.S. certifying agency. In the case of one type of jet airliner, for example, it was the British air safety registration board that caused the manufacturer to add some structural protection—which was only gradually retrofitted to aircraft sold in the United States.

When there are no codes in existence, design is governed by basic principles of engineering, materials guidebooks, and factors of safety. What the plaintiff engineer regards as poor design and violations of good practice will most probably be defended as good practice equally strenuously by the engineers working for the defense. It is out of such conflicts that hard-fought jury trials are generated. But if good practice has been compromised for dollar savings on the part of the manufacturer, the plaintiff might not have to fight very hard to win his case.

---

* Industry procedures in setting standards have been attacked by the National Commission on Product Safety and many other consumer organizations.

Many attorneys agree that in the majority of cases, errors in design are simple things that "just should not have been overlooked." They would not have been if the manufacturer had used a good design-review process. Competent designers will carefully check strengths, weights, etc., on all *major* parts of a machine or process. But less important parts frequently get shortchanged.

Sometimes, also, a safety feature will be deleted from a machine or product at the very last stage of production to effect a reduction in cost, weight, or volume, or because of a temporary parts shortage that is being sanctified by a change in design. A safety feature may be added at the request of sales personnel ("to meet the competition") but on an optional, extra-cost basis. The unwitting customer who fails to ask, or who shops price, gets the product sans options.

A good design-review process would force the mandatory incorporation of safety devices to guard against foreseeable dangers, as determined by a standard of reasonable care and prudence. The nature of such a standard is discussed throughout this book. For our purposes here, suffice it to say that just as liability law is an evolving mechanism, so is the standard: What is reasonable care today will not be so ten years hence, as society becomes more complex and its members owe one another a greater duty of care.

Construction. Failures in construction often involve some production error, although sometimes a construction fault indicates lack of careful design as well. Construction errors are especially damaging to a firm when it can be proved that one type of bolt was substituted for another or one type of material changed to another without approval from the design personnel and appropriate documentation. Such substitutions are usually made because of pressures to keep an assembly line operating in the face of certain parts or material shortages. Paperwork fails to keep up, and the plaintiff attorney points a damaging finger. The individual who approved the substitution will eventually find himself in an uncomfortable witness chair if he failed to get approval from design.

A construction failure may also result from an error in assembly by a worker or from the failure of a machine to insert a needed part, such as a cotter pin to hold a nut in place. (In the latter case, the plaintiff attorney may charge the manufacturer with a design defect as well: "You should have had a backup for such an assembly contingency.")

Inspection. A great many defects investigated in product liability cases contain elements of an inspection failure. The omission of a cable clamp in a strategic area, the upside-down insertion of a bearing in a machine tool, the incorporation of an obviously faulty switch—all these, the plaintiff attorney will say, could have been "easily prevented had the firm inspected its components and its production processes." Sampling plans, with their implicit acceptance of some percentage of defects getting through the process, will often take a pounding in front of a jury [8]—unless the defense attorney can prove that sampling was the only feasible way to maintain the production line and that the plan used was expertly designed, competently executed, and under continuous professional review.

As we noted in Chapter 1, the defect which does get through and which does cause bodily injury makes the manufacturer strictly liable in tort. In such a case, the engineer will not stop with simply proving such a defect. He will try to show negligence as well, in order to make his case more impressive to the jury and permit recovery for economic consequential damages if applicable.

The plaintiff attorney will remind the jury that there are techniques (researched by the engineer for him) that would have picked up the obvious (patent) and even the hidden (latent) defects. The attorney will argue that since the defect which caused the accident was present in the product when it left the plant, as demonstrated by the engineer's investigation, it is "obvious" that the firm's inspection procedures were faulty and the firm was negligent. It is easy for the plaintiff engineer to come up with techniques by which a particuar defect could have been caught by inspection, because he is looking at the situation after the fact—he knows where the defect was, what kind it was, and what it caused. In front of the jury he projects himself backwards in time to the production of the item in question and testifies that the firm, had it done what he now suggests, would have found the defect. This implies that the suggested inspection was warranted and that the firm simply failed to carry it out. Such testimony is extremely effective with a jury of unsophisticated laymen. (And, as will be explained in a later chapter, a smart attorney—whether he represents the plaintiff or the defendant—keeps technically sophisticated people *off* the jury.)

Testing. In some situations the deficiency in the product is attributable to a lack of testing before the product was released onto the market. A product should be tested to do the job it is supposed to do: It should be tested not just as a design proto-type but as a production model, and not just for highly visible, sales-oriented characteristics but for its ability to operate safely under the worst environmental conditions foreseeable and (in some cases) with a stupid, irresponsible operator doing stupid, irresponsible things. In some industries the latter is a common modus operandi, and might therefore be labeled "reasonably foreseeable misuse and abuse."

The company must guard against reasonably foreseeable un-intended use as well as reasonably foreseeable misuse and abuse. The precautions taken against reasonably foreseeable misuse range from the extremely strict ones in the toy industry to the much looser expectations applied to trained professionals who, presumably, know what they are doing when using a product. In a consumer product, especially, if the action sequence was misuse–failure–accident, then the plaintiff attorney will tell the jury that product failure caused the accident and the company was negligent. The defendant attorney will tell the jury that product misuse caused the accident. The jury's conclusion will depend on the skill each side demonstrates in proving its point, but the plaintiff, with a damaged product as evidence, often has a decided advantage. In an industrial situation, by contrast, there will often be witnesses who can testify to the degree of misuse, if any, displayed by the user of a machine or product. Here the user is supposed to be trained and informed regarding that product, so the defendant stands a better chance of getting off the hook. This is particularly true where the state of the art with certain machines simply does not admit of 100 percent protection against accident (i.e., no hazard or risk) without diminishing drastically the economic usefulness of the machine.

The plaintiff engineer seeks a mismatch between what the product should have been able to withstand and what it did withstand (which, of course, led to the failure). By inductive reasoning the engineer may decide that inadequate testing was the possible cause of failure. He or she can then advise the plaintiff attorney to thoroughly investigate the firm's testing practices. A riding mower may never have been tested on hills, or tests on children's toys may have been run only by careful, highly competent adults. When a product liability suit is imminent, a thorough engineer never fails to investigate the mental-physical characteristics of the operators and the question of whether the product should have withstood adverse environmental conditions.

Warning. Producers owe it to their customers to reduce to a minimum all possible risks involved in the use of a product— including the chance that product failure will cause an accident. After they have done this to the best of their ability, they must warn the customer of all remaining risks involved in the use of the product. The warning must be conveyed in a manner that will penetrate the consciousness of the customer or operator and guide his actions accordingly. For example, if a poisonous product is sold in an area where people are illiterate, or might by some remote possibility be brought into such an area, some mark, sign, symbol, or other device must communicate "poison" to the user. If children are liable to get their hands on the product, the warning responsibility becomes that much greater for the firm. Is it a dishwashing detergent that looks like a bottle of milk? One large, well-known firm was test marketing just such a product when the FDA seized field samples and forced a change in packaging. The principal author's three-year-old son was caught sucking on a bottle of green hair tonic formulated with a hefty percentage of denatured alcohol. The author tasted it too; it was deliciously sweet! Since the tonic was so palatable, a special warning to keep it away from children would have been in order—or a bitter substance could have been added to its formula.

Does the label give complete information regarding intended use, and does it communicate to all potential users all possible negative effects? Of course, post-accident 20/20 hindsight helps the engineer provide the attorney with a good account of what was left out of the warning, and later the jury is made to feel that the company was negligent in not having had 20/20 foresight. A good plaintiff attorney does not have to work very hard to demonstrate that a company with resources to dream up a product and move it to market should also have the prescience to warn against the problem the plaintiff suffered.

There is a famous case of a glue which gives off explosive vapors (now being replaced on the market by non-explosive glue). The label said, in very small print, that the product should be "used with adequate ventilation." A carpenter using the glue to install a new kitchen countertop was badly hurt when a nearby stove pilot light ignited the vapors. The jury agreed that the label should have recommended ventilation by forced air (fan) and extinguishing all nearby flames. A very large award to the plaintiff was the result; the firm had failed to inform the user about the product's dangers.

The duty to warn against hazards was given further dimensions by a recent U.S. Supreme Court decision upholding an award to the widow of a worker who died of lung cancer.[9] The man had been exposed to asbestos dust from 1936 to 1969 while working as an insulation installer. He sued the suppliers of the material, not his employer, and won a landmark decision. The Court held that even though the asbestos was the only known product suitable for the use to which it was being put over the years of his injury, the suppliers were liable because the link between disease and material was established before the man began work and he was not warned of the dangers. The Court held that an insulation worker has the same right as any other product user to be warned of the hazards of the product he is handling and that the warning must be explicit so the worker understands it. This decision opens up a whole new line of attack for plaintiff attorneys in industrial health cases.

The essential point which the engineer seeks to prove is that the firm failed to adequately communicate needed information to all those who would be in contact with the product and might suffer damages from it. If the firm's message was not understood, it is not the intellectual capacity of the injured party that will be questioned, but rather the communicator's "demonstrated lack of effort to communicate."

Res Ipsa Loquitur

The second concept which the engineer uses for building an attack on the firm's product is the doctrine of *res ipsa loquitur*— which, as we noted earlier, is roughly translated as "the thing speaks for itself." The engineer proves—by use of demonstration models or through careful reasoning—that an accident could not have taken place without something having failed. By inference, the failure would not have happened if the people who handled the product along the stream of commerce had not been negligent in some way. Thus, in a *res ipsa* case the engineer shows how "good" the normal or fault-free product is and then turns his attack to how negligent the firm was in permitting an obvious defect to get through.

Given a choice among retailer, distributor, and manufacturer as primary targets for a suit, the plaintiff attorney will usually try to show that the negligence was at the manufacturer level, claiming that the accident would not have happened if there had not been a failure in design, construction, inspection, testing, or warning. The retailer and distributor, who want to avoid responsibility for the damages, will help shift the blame to the manufacturer. *Res ipsa* is especially appropriate in a situation where the article that caused the problem was destroyed beyond recognition. In many cases, however, it is a tough doctrine for the plaintiff attorney to use because the defendant can raise the issue that mishandling of the product outside its doors created the accident-causing condition. The blame could lie, the manufacturer will say, with virtually anyone who came in contact with the product in the stream of commerce. Industrial cases in which different contractors handle shipping, installation, assembly, and testing are examples of the ultimate diffusion of responsibility that can occur.

To illustrate the use of *res ipsa* in a consumer situation, consider the case where a grinding wheel exploded and caused the loss of a man's eye. *Res ipsa* was demonstrated: An undamaged or fault-free grinding wheel, when properly used by the customer, does not explode. But the defendant firm convinced the jury to shift a large proportion of the damage settlement onto the ultimate retailer in the case, because the retailer could just as easily have dropped or mishandled the wheel prior to delivery to the customer. The small, uninsured retailer declared bankruptcy and the plaintiff never collected very much from him.

No matter how the engineer handles his report, his objective remains as stated previously: Demonstrate, with ironclad proof, what caused the accident and prove that all other causes are unfeasible.

An Eye to the Jury

The reader has probably noticed our constant references to the effect of the engineer's work on the jury.* The plaintiff attorney and his engineer evaluate everything they do in terms of its ultimate effect on the jury. They judge the strength of the plaintiff's case not in terms of legal theories (though these cannot be sloppily put together) but in terms of how the case will look when presented to a jury. The engineer's work might consist of the most brilliantly derived stress graphs ever seen in a courtroom, but they do not strengthen the case unless they make specific, clear, and impressive points for the jury to consider. The converse may also occur: Some weak investigations cover themselves with impressive-looking graphs.

An astute defendant will keep in mind this orientation of the plaintiff attorney and build his or her responses accordingly.

The Engineer's Fee

The plaintiff engineer's fee is usually paid by the attorney with a check drawn by the client—which brings us to the interesting question of fees. Various sums are bandied about as "reasonable"

* If both sides agree, they may waive their right to trial by jury and allow the trial to go forward before a judge. But this decision is usually not made until the last minute before the trial, and therefore both attorneys must base their preparations on the assumption of trial by jury.

fees for the engineer, but realities do not follow a set script. The fee often bears little relation to the complexity of the case. The reputation of the engineer determines the starting point, with the negotiating range being from $175 to $400 per day. Then the client's pocketbook comes into account. For a case with a well-to-do client, the attorney will agree to a high fee. Where the client is a poor working person or a marginal business, negotiations become uncomfortable; the attorney needs good work but at a price the client can afford. The engineer would be violating his code of ethics if he were to work on a contingency fee basis and wait for the plaintiff to win his case. If the engineer wants additional work from this attorney or referrals to other attorneys, he may wind up subsidizing a complex case by investing his energies at a low rate now because of expected higher rates in future cases.

In this regard, the corporate defendant and his insurance firm have a huge advantage—they have the funds to pay anyone they need and so can get the best talent available. The engineering consultant who has an insurance company for a client can generally spend far more lavishly for tests, high-speed movies, and ancillary support in his investigations than when working for citizen John Doe. In some cases a defendant firm can even tap a competitor's staff for an expert at no cost—especially when loss of a particular case will make the whole industry vulnerable.

Choosing the Consultant

The attorney who buys the expertise of a consultant owes it to his or her client to check the consultant's references: How well did the engineer handle previous reports he did, and how well did he conduct his courtroom testimony in previous cases? This is, of course, in addition to reviewing his general professional background, education, teaching experience (if any), reading habits, professional memberships, and experience relating to the product under investigation.

Most plaintiff engineers have very precise and narrow qualifications with strong reputations in particular types of cases. However, some engineers are adept at claiming expertise for a multitude of products by implying that any given product is simply a construct of "generally recognized engineering principles"—with which, of course, they are thoroughly familiar. For these plaintiff engineers, it's not what you know but how you present it that counts. There have been situations where defendant firm engineers sat in the courtroom and listened to such "qualified" people spew a stream of verbal garbage about the product to the jury, and then heard the jury reward the plaintiff with a hefty settlement. To refute these people demands more than sheer technical expertise.

As more college professors enter the liability field, their expertise will become increasingly available to plaintiff attorneys. Since most professors view the income as purely supplementary to their teaching salaries, their fees are lower. Furthermore, the college professor often makes use of his or her school's laboratory equipment at zero cost—a saving that can also be passed on to the client.

In the best of all worlds, the professional engineer who assists the plaintiff attorney would demonstrate extremely good skills in investigating an accident, writing a report, and testifying in court. The first requires having served an apprenticeship with someone in the field (you can't learn to investigate from a book), the second requires writing ability (evidenced by prior reports and papers written), and the third a bit of ham. The top negligence attorneys are unusually good at sizing up a person along all three dimensions and rarely lose a case because of their engineer's shortcomings. The more successful an attorney is and the bigger his reputation, the greater his choice of experts and, not so paradoxically, the less he might have to pay for engineering support on a particular case. He promises repeat business and referrals.

THE NEXT LEGAL STEP: THE COMPLAINT

As soon as the engineer communicates to the attorney that he has proof of negligence relating to the cause of the accident (sometimes even before the engineer's full report is prepared), the attorney prepares a legal complaint document. He aims this complaint at every party who had any connection whatsoever with the product, from birth to construction to sale to service to inspection. Even the person who advised or consulted on the purchase of the particular device may be named, especially in industrial cases. As the chain is traced back to the manufacturer, individual engineers, designers, draftsmen, quality control people, assemblers, and all supervisors will sooner or later be identified and added to the complaint. It stands to reason that the plaintiff attorney does not hope to win much money from any of these individuals, but as they defend themselves they will help prove his case of corporate negligence, and that is where the jackpot lies. Occasionally the chain of involvement extends back to one of the manufacturer's vendors, but this is not too common. The plaintiff attorney leaves it to the manufacturer to recover from his vendor on his own if a damage settlement has been won for the injured party.

The reasoning behind "sue everybody" bears repetition because of its extreme importance to both the plaintiff and the defense: As each of the parties seeks dismissal of the case against himself, or mitigation of exposure to damages during the jury trial, the plaintiff sits with a "no-lose" situation—someone is going to say or do something that will help his case. In some multiple-defendant cases, the mutual attacks the defendants make upon one another assure the plaintiff attorney a judgment far in excess of what he might otherwise have gotten from the jury.

It is relatively easy to trace the history of a consumer product. The retailer usually reveals the identity of his distributor as soon as he is alerted by the plaintiff attorney that litigation is pending; a simple telephone call is sufficient. The distributor readily identifies the manufacturer. Later on, the identities of the designers and other manufacturing personnel become known when the attorney gains access to drawings, memoranda, and production orders.

Some distributors package goods, or claim they test the product, or alter its container by overprinting, or put in (and sometimes leave out) instruction sheets—they increase their potential liability accordingly. If the product is a foreign-made item imported and handled by a distributor (and the foreign manufacturer is not a "fat," visible target here in the United States), then the distributor becomes the prime target in the suit and all the faults previously discussed are attributed to him.

Retailers often assemble or sell a device "off the floor" that has unknowingly been damaged by careless individuals who handled the display. The retailer becomes liable for not having inspected and tested the device to make sure it was completely without fault.

A distributor or retailer who becomes aware of a product defect through industry scuttlebutt or self-discovery, or who should have been aware by reason of actual or claimed expertise and still sells the product, also becomes a party to demonstrated negligence. Certain distributors and retailers are big enough to be fat targets for liability suits. If the plaintiff attorney has reason to believe that they had knowledge of a defect, it becomes worth his while to hire an investigator. The investigator may find a disgruntled employee to corroborate the attorney's beliefs. If the employee held a supervisory position with the firm, and particularly if he has some written memos that he conveniently kept with him after his departure, he can make a great deal of trouble for the firm. Again, a corollary: The firm with managers party to sensitive information should treat them in a humane fashion, especially should separation become necessary. In the event the firm becomes a liability suit defendant, an ex-employee with a grudge against the firm may bring up information which helps impeach the firm's general credibility or gives new leads to the plaintiff attorney.

Each defendant party is usually accused of at least one specific negligent act. But to allow future expansion of the allegations as more information becomes available, the plaintiff attorney always includes in his or her complaint some phraseology labeling the defendant's actions "otherwise careless and negligent under the circumstances."

The complaint, delivered to the secretary of the corporation or the merchant in his store, sometimes is the first indication a defendant has of the impending suit. Complaints are immediately turned over to the defending insurance firm or attorney. These parties usually respond with a complete denial of all charges. Some defending attorneys, whether or not they work for an insurance firm, have such denials virtually ready to go, and need only fill in the pertinent details of the case at hand.

THE BILL OF PARTICULARS

The plaintiff attorney's next salvo is a bill of particulars (which the defendant attorney may have requested when sending the denial mentioned above). Filing this with the defendant corporation completes the first major stage of the actual suit process.

The function of the bill of particulars is to amplify the complaint by providing a detailed personal history of the injured party, up to and through the accident (or commercial disaster), plus every human mental and physical cost (or business cost) measured in every conceivable way into the distant future. Claims are made for all manner of losses, to justify a demand for large monetary compensation. This information, of course, will come out in court later on, and the attorney preparing the bill of particulars must be careful not to limit himself. He will be accused of exaggeration no matter how much he claims. If he claims too little, however, he will never recover from this initial mistake, even if additional information developed during the suit reveals far greater injury or commercial damage than was previously suspected.

Oftentimes, a defendant firm manager reviewing a bill of particulars with his attorneys wonders how the injured party's residential history is relevant to a lost limb. Or he may wonder how a firm's relations with a "famous customer" can bear on the loss of its commercial flower bed. The plaintiff attorney will use the residential history to show how impressive the stature of the injured party was before the accident, because his company "promoted and moved him several times up the executive ladder." The flower bed company "had a fabulous business going," proved by its service to that famous person before the accident. The information gathered, however, can be a two-edged sword. The defendant attorney will counter by referring to "the shiftlessness of a man who moves eight times in nine years," or by saying "How secure could a business be when its existence hangs on service to one 'famous customer'?"

The information in the bill of particulars is used to determine how much a person or business was worth, over a lifetime, before the accident occurred. Economic specialists aid attorneys in performing the necessary calculations. They use actuarial tables, calculations of total monetary earnings, conversion of a number of factors into dollar terms (e.g., worth to the family of a father or mother, worth to the community of an outstanding contributor), and anything else they can find relevant in judging the worth of a person. For a business that has been damaged, discounted cash flow and other techniques are applied to a projected earnings stream. The amount arrived at is compared with "the drastic reduction in all of these" as a result of the accident for which monetary compensation is sought. In severe personal injury cases, a detailed listing of the medical bills can often take up several pages of the bill of particulars—which can be, in its entirety, dozens of pages long. Commercial cases involving loss of business and contracts that cannot be honored because of the accident lead to very long bills of particulars.

QUESTIONING AND EXAMINATION

The next stage in the legal proceedings amounts to a mutual probing of weaknesses and strengths by each side. The idea is for the opposing sides to ask each other questions and examine the product and all related evidence.

There will usually be some jockeying back and forth as to who goes first in questioning and examination. The side that goes last in questioning all witnesses and parties to the accident sometimes makes huge gains on the basis of information uncovered in previous questioning. In the case of examination, however, both sides fight to get to the product and related evidence first. The wise plaintiff attorney makes absolutely sure that whenever possible he seizes control of the evidence first. (This may be difficult if his client tipped off the company defendant by a prior contact.) He should then never relinquish control over the evidence until the plaintiff engineer has thoroughly examined it from every possible viewpoint. In some cases the plaintiff engineer has to literally chop the product to pieces to thoroughly examine it. What happens when the defendant eventually gets to examine a product that is now a "box of scrap" will be covered in a later chapter.

Questioning can take place in one of two ways—by interrogatory or by deposition.

The Interrogatory

In some states and federal courts, the prevailing method is the interrogatory. Interrogatories are written requests for information. They may be sent by either side, but are most often used by the attorneys for the defendant firm's insurance company to question the plaintiff in depth. An interrogatory can have anywhere from 100 to 300 questions, each of which may have parts (a), (b), (c), and so on. Many a defendant firm manager has been hit with a request by his firm's attorneys to list all possible details he would ask about in an accident situation involving the firm's product. Some managers treat this request as a nuisance intrusion into their daily work, but the attorneys really need this information. To make up a truly complete interrogatory, they also need information gathered from others in the firm, prior similar cases, cooperating competitors, insurance records, and other research.

After a few cases involving a particular product line, the attorneys for the defense may wind up with a "boiler plate" interrogatory containing many questions that will be irrelevant in particular cases. These are used to cover every conceivable detail that could be even remotely related to a product liability case. There are obvious cost savings in using the same form over and over again. In addition, if he so desires, the attorney can turn to publications which will give him—lock, stock, and barrel —entire interrogations tailored to fit virtually every type of product.[10] The publications show both kinds of interrogatories: those from defendant to plaintiff and those from plaintiff to defendant.

The company manager who is interested in doing an offbeat audit of how well his firm is performing in product liability prevention could well profit from using both types of forms to construct a checklist of penetrating questions to ask his people.

When a firm is having labor problems, or an ex-employee can be reached, it is often worthwhile for the plaintiff attorney to send an investigator to frequent worker bars and steer the conversation to company quality control operations, particularly any differences between company manuals and actual operations procedures. Some of the specificities hit by the plaintiff's resulting interrogatory to the firm sometimes cause acute embarassment up and down management ranks.

An interrogatory prepared by the plaintiff attorney can ask for drawings, reports, memos, and all kinds of background information; it is limited virtually only by the imagination and experience of the propounder. Many negligence attorneys have developed boiler-plate interrogatories themselves, and the manager of the defendant firm finds himself cursing dozens of seemingly irrelevant questions. Be careful; they are a trap! Just as much care must be taken in answering an irrelevant question as one which seems directly pertinent, lest the plaintiff attorney be supplied with an unexpected quarter of attack.

Interrogatories are usually transmitted by mail and sworn to by the familiar processes of signature and notarizing. The advantages in using them, where not required by a specific state's courts, are cost savings in preparation (especially with boiler-plate forms) and elimination of the need for attorneys and witnesses to meet at appointed times and places. The main disadvantage is that the attorney for the recipient has much time to think of his answers, can call in as many people as he wants to help formulate the "right" answers, and can then review their answers carefully before having the interrogatory signed. This is chiefly a disadvantage to the plaintiff: The plaintiff attorney usually works only with the injured party and his engineer, while the attorney for the corporate insurer can marshal a whole army of helpers. A further disadvantage of the interrogatory is that badly worded questions usually elicit badly worded answers, which might miss crucial points. Sometimes an attorney does not even realize that his question is badly propounded or badly worded or just, by its nature, gives the other party a way out of an embarrassing situation by deflecting attention to other matters.

The Deposition

The more favored but very expensive method is the taking of a deposition; it is used in addition to a bill of particulars and an interrogatory, rarely in place of them. A deposition is a face-to-face encounter between an attorney and a witness, with stenographic recording of the sworn testimony. Here, the questions are being propounded as the answers are received. The attorney may be working from a boiler-plate outline, but his powers of observation or his "sixth sense" will lead him to propound questions on the spot whenever he notices even the least weakness in a witness's statements. A good, experienced deposition attorney can pick up a contradiction in statements from even the slightest nuances. And he zeroes in before the witness even has a chance to realize what he has done. Depositions also give the attorney a chance to evaluate the witness's potential impact on a jury should the case go to trial. An impressive witness can strengthen his side of the case to an important degree.

Depositions can be a rough experience for a witness, because his attorney cannot respond for him and sometimes a blurted remark can be quite damaging. His attorney is present to defend him against trick questions or to force clarifications of peculiarly worded questions, but after that the witness is on his own.

Examination of Evidence

The plaintiff attorney, especially in extremely high-value cases, will go to any lengths to obtain everything even remotely connected with the product and the operations of the firm. This includes everything from memos to notebooks to personal diaries. The defendant seeks protection from the court on the grounds that the plaintiff does not know what he is doing and is on a hunt-and-fish expedition to pry into trade secrets. Such protection is rarely granted. In the words of one major defense attorney, "the company better have a damn good reason for restricting a trade secret [from plaintiff's eyes]" before it even considers asking for court protection.

This hunt-and-fish process comes under the attorney's right of "broad discovery." The plaintiff attorney and his engineer descend upon the firm, where they can order up any and all records —from design to production to shipping to service to scrapping —and can physically examine every inch of the factory floor and laboratories.

Does this probing pay off? We answer by citing a drug case in which an attorney spent three days at the manufacturer's plant. The attorney examined records showing how the drug progressed from original inception, how it was synthesized from a natural state, and how it underwent FDA processes, as well as all reports from the field and all controls for field testing. Production facilities were visited and operations records were inspected.

This drug had a known side effect that could be as devastating as the diseases it was designed to cure. The side effect was so well known that the company published warnings and directed use of the drug only as a last-ditch defense against insidious diseases such as typhoid or rocky mountain spotted fever. Only a small number of cases per year are reported, worldwide, for these diseases. Total requirements for treatment of all cases: one pound of the drug per year.

The actual production was in *tons*, and the drug contributed one-third of the company's income.

An intensive investigation was triggered by the contradiction between requirements and production. Company detail men had been verbally telling the doctors to disregard the warnings and use the drug for a broad panoply of problems as a first line of defense. A doctor's malpractice suit became a company-negligence, punitive-damages situation, and the firm (and its insurer) took a terrible beating.

The key point here is that the information leading to the destruction of the company's defense would not have been available had depositions been taken in an attorney's office or in a distant city. When depositions are taken at the plant, leads uncovered by questions can immediately be followed up by discovery proceedings, such as requests for documents or immediate examination of a production facility.

Deposition-taking goes from the highest management levels down to the lowest levels of the defendant firm, and across every department. As was previously mentioned, printed operational procedures may in fact represent only a shadow of what actually goes on in a plant. Exposure of deviations will not be lost on a jury.

The defendant firm's countermove should also be mentioned. When the plaintiff attorney shows up at the plant and asks broad questions, he gets broad answers—and, literally, a carload of paper.[11] In the Corvair litigation, attorney Richard Markus tells us, GM's response to requests for production records was "We have available two large file rooms . . . for your inspection." Another case that Markus handled yielded 75 file cabinets for inspection. The discouraging aspects of this are obvious, and only careful preplanning prevents this inundation from choking the plaintiff's mission.

If no reports are available, or if the company destroyed certain design, production, or test records after several years, or if written operations procedures do not exist, the plaintiff may build a substantial part of his case on this point alone. In court, the plaintiff attorney will repeatedly call for records and procedures he knows do not exist and will then remind the jury that "a responsible firm keeps records," or "only an irresponsible management operates without a procedures manual." If the records were destroyed, "it is pretty obvious to us all that there must have been something damaging in them."

A corollary for the defendant firm: The company is best off keeping the aforementioned records—and keeping them in an unexpurgated form. A bad record can be explained away or mitigating circumstances can be introduced. If records are kept but purged of negative items, their purity makes them highly suspect.

Interrogatories, depositions, investigations under the broad-discovery concept, and/or research continues until both sides feel they have extracted everything they can from the other. The plaintiff sets up his case to attack the product and all who brought it to market (or even advised a client to use it), while the defendants set up to demolish all the allegations.

Parties to court actions often ask about the accuracy and truthfulness of all the sworn statements and discovery items. Most attorneys agree that company people do not commit perjury. They may try to slant testimony to present their actions in the best possible light, but going beyond this is believed to be quite rare. Perjury on the behalf of the plaintiff might happen in some cases, but definitely not many. It is extremely risky for an attorney to go any further than channeling his client's testimony along broad outlines he has developed. It is difficult to remember a fabricated story under good cross-examination, and perjury is almost sure to result in loss of the case—even a good case.

Once all information is on hand, the outlines of the case are pretty much established, and all evidence has been secured, the case is put on the court calendar for trial. The time elapsed between the client's first contact with his attorney and setting a date for trial could be years; three and four are not unusual numbers.

In the next chapter we will jump to the defendant's side of the fence and review his actions in depth—with, of course, special attention to the role of management. In later chapters we will bring the two sides together, detail the extensive settlement negotiations that have been going on from, literally, the beginning of the suit, and discuss the intensive trial-preparation work and the trial itself.

REFERENCES

1. Dean A. Robb, Harry M. Philo, and Richard M. Goodman, *Lawyers Desk Reference,* 4th ed. (Rochester, N.Y.: Lawyers Cooperative Publishing Company, 1971), Appendix A.
2. Ibid., p. x.
3. Two sources that offer a broad survey of product-liability-related

accident investigations are Louis R. Frumer and Melvin I. Friedman, *Products Liability* (New York: Matthew Bender, 1971);
and George A. Peters, *Product Liability and Safety* (Washington,
D.C.: Coiner Publications, 1971).

4. Harry M. Philo, "Sources of Information: Finding the Expert."
   ATL Counseling Cassettes, Vol. 4, No. 7, Association of Trial
   Lawyers of America, 1974.
5. Ibid.
6. Frumer and Friedman, op. cit., par. 7.01.
7. Ibid.
8. Frumer and Friedman, op. cit., have a superb section on sampling
   plans and the outcomes of cases involving such plans. We also
   refer the reader to our comments on grain sampling in Chapter 1.
9. "A Large Liability for Unsafe Employers," *Business Week* (October 26, 1974), pp. 42–44. See also Alan Anderson, Jr., "The
   "Hidden Plague," *The New York Times Magazine* (October 27,
   1974), pp. 20ff.
10. *Bender's Forms of Discovery VIIIA, Products Liability* (New
    York: Matthew Bender Company, 1973); and *American Juris-
    prudence Proof of Facts* (Rochester, N.Y.: Lawyers Cooperative
    Publishing Company, 1961). Both publications are kept up to
    date by the issuance of supplements.
11. Richard M. Markus, "The Discovery Tools." *ATL Counseling
    Cassettes*, Vol. 4, No. 2, Association of Trial Lawyers of America,
    1974.

3

MAKING READY
FOR
THE DEFENSE

Too many managers are under the misapprehension that their insurance underwriter and its battalions of attorneys determine their firm's response to product liability claims. In actual fact, two aspects of policy set by top management are the key parameters. They involve (1) the firm's view of profits, and (2) its attitude toward lawsuits. In this chapter we will review these parameters and then go on to show how they shape the defense of a product liability suit. We hope this information will help the reader to appropriately shape his or her inputs to the management hierarchy when trying to do some liability prevention. To put it bluntly: A giant, monopolistic, customer-be-damned firm is not likely to respond to a manager's suggestions until it has been severely burned by liability suits or strong consumerist actions.

THE COMPANY'S ATTITUDE TOWARD PROFITS [1]

Management's view of profits sets the tone for how all echelons of the firm respond to defective products and handle the resultant law suits. Profit may be viewed as:

1. A reward for bearing risks and uncertainties. (Risk is differentiated from uncertainty by the fact that probabilities can be determined for the former, but not for the latter.)
2. A consequence of imperfections in the competitive, dynamic marketplace.
3. A reward for successful innovation.

Under the risk-and-uncertainty doctrine, return on investment is the key to all decisions. The minimum investment needed for a targeted cash flow must result in profits that yield a rate of return better than that of any alternative investment. The way to save on this investment is to put as few funds as possible into any function that can be considered non-line and non-revenue-producing. And the way to reduce operating costs is to make the smallest possible budgetary allowances to non-line, non-revenue-producing functions. If customer service, quality control, and research, for example, are considered non-line, non-revenue-producing entities, it stands to reason that these functions will be limited. Liability prevention plays little or no part in decision making beyond shifting the risks to the insurance carrier.

The second mode of thought about profits delves into the concept of imperfections in competition. The loosest example may be that of a chain outlet in a ghetto. This outlet might charge more for its products than a sister store in a different (perhaps wealthier) neighborhood because the latter's customers are more mobile and will unhesitatingly drive long distances for better values. The ghetto store takes advantage of the immobility of the ghetto residents. In a similar fashion, the manufacturer (or distributor or retailer) who believes profits are a function of imperfections in the marketplace will constantly be striving to reduce competition, increase patent protection, and control the resources for the production, distribution, and sales of his product. Such a management tries to achieve a market position whereby customers are presented with a take-it-or-leave-it choice with regard to an entire class of goods or services. Only rarely, in such a situation, are the user's real needs and expectations taken into consideration by the firm's decision makers.

The third broad class of profit seekers sees profitability as a function of innovation. A firm concerned with discovering new ideas in a research laboratory and converting them into marketable and producible products (the scientific transfer process [2]) must inevitably make consideration of the user integral to all its activities. As Lorsch points out, "Trade shows, industry shows, and the informal flow of information throughout the industry keep the researchers advised of changes . . . in competitors' products." [3] The marketing function deals with the complexity of customer problems and constantly changing customer needs, as well as pressures created by the active innovation programs of competitors.[4] The production unit must meet the demands imposed as new or modified processes are developed; a high degree of integration is needed between research and production so that the former develops a feasible process and the latter adopts the new process smoothly into its operations.[5]

Businesses genuinely concerned with innovation as the key to profits almost inevitably are extremely customer-oriented. These two quotes exemplify the management viewpoint in such companies:

> In its commitment to customer service IBM learned that the best way to serve a prospect was to provide equipment adapted to his requirements, rather than ask him to alter his business to fit our needs.[6]
>
> THOMAS J. WATSON, JR.
> *Former Chairman of the Board, IBM*

> . . . At all levels of production and distribution (with innovations in the latter) the key question in the minds of those concerned is how closely a given product will interpret correctly the customer's balance between his interest in price, quality, utility, life, and dependability.[7]
>
> THEODORE V. HOUSER
> *Chairman, Sears, Roebuck & Co.*

No business operates from any one profit viewpoint for all operating decisions up and down the entire managerial hierarchy. However, the long-term stress of top management on one particular belief is extremely important in determining how much "service" the user or consumer of the firm's output gets. In our context, it is also a fundamental determinant of the manner in which the firm responds to customer complaints.

The risk-profiter takes a cost/benefit approach to customer service. Among the firms practicing this philosophy are large and powerful marketers of name-brand products. They carefully watch the cost of increased quality (fewer rejects or returns) versus the cost of litigation and strike a balance at the lowest total cost. They spread insurance costs and risks to multiple firms through, for example, franchising self-insurance for all but catastrophic events, or simply through layers of corporate holding companies.

Companies with the cost/benefit approach resist a complaint in direct proportion to its size. Generally, small complaints are bought off by a quick product exchange. Larger complaints are resisted fairly strongly up to a predetermined settlement value. If the customer acquiesces, he gets that settlement—otherwise he is fought to the bitter end.

Implicit in this approach is the assumption of steady customer acceptance of the brand. But companies can no longer depend on consumer loyalty in the face of damaging tales from those who suffer, or consumer optimism regarding government reaction to multiple complaints. Furthermore, this approach entirely overlooks the very real possibility of insurance cancellation.

It was mentioned above that risk-oriented firms sometimes protect themselves through layers of corporate holding companies. The layer concept is used by firms with weak or cancelled insurance and an inability to underwrite their exposure through the internal mechanisms we will discuss in Chapter 5. The assets of the firm will be endangered in any liability action. Therefore, several corporations are formed: one which owns the factory building, another which owns all the machinery, another which owns the inventory, and so on. All lease their services to a parent firm which is a financial shell easily bankrupted in the event of a large damage award. At one major airline virtually all the aircraft engines were owned by one leasing company, all the aircraft were owned by several others, and the overhaul base by still others. While in this case liability protection may have played only a small part in establishing such a structure, it illustrates how a layering concept can exist even in big-name companies.

A variation of the layer concept is used by firms that lease production machinery with "hold harmless" clauses in the lease. In such contracts, the owning firm, not the operating firm, trains the operators, maintains the devices, and is totally responsible for any workmen's compensation and product liability suits. Again, while the initial impetus for such leasing contracts may have come from financial and tax considerations, there is no doubt that many executives are glad to have injuries in the plant "become the headache of the other guy." (The Occupational Safety and Health Act has had a beneficial effect in holding operators' managers to a less casual attitude toward job safety.)

In some cases, the supplier does not wish to become involved in such an arrangement. He therefore sells parts or even major components to a specially set up assembly corporation (whose nameplate goes on the device), with all kinds of liability protection written into the contracts between them so as to protect the supplier. This corporation, in turn, sells or leases the device to the ultimate user. If a worker is injured and a suit is brought against the firm whose nameplate is on the device, it is for all practical purposes a shell corporation that will absorb the major impact. Of course, knowledgeable plaintiff attorneys will attack the supplier at the beginning of the chain, as well as all the others, but in some circumstances where the attorney has not done his homework he finds himself with a judgment against the shell, which has been deliberately underinsured and is easily bankrupted.

The manager with the market-imperfection philosophy may also try to buy off small claims—often to avoid publicity and exposure of his operation to consumer groups. He fights hard against larger claims and, especially on the retail level, may operate in hand with a finance company to maintain billing pressure even if the merchandise is subpar. The innovator, by contrast, reaches forward to help the user or consumer of his product and will go to great lengths to see to it that customer dissatisfaction is mitigated, even at great expense to his firm.

It is the informal opinion of many attorneys that firms which tend to take cosmetic approaches to consumer complaints invite more serious actions than those which truly "care." The message should now be clear: A company's profit philosophy determines its response to the need for product quality; this in turn determines its response to complaints, which in turn influences the volume of suits. Thus many suits can be clipped at the source by caring for the customer. In terms of the equilateral triangle which we discussed in Chapter 1—with apexes representing quality, quantity, and cost—those firms which flatten the triangle and pay as much attention to quality as the other two parameters suffer fewer suits of less serious nature than others which put quality down.

THE COMPANY'S ATTITUDE TOWARD LAWSUITS

The second key parameter is the firm's attitude toward suits. Most companies decide to make nuisance-value claim settlements quickly.* Some companies will buy off suits under a given figure just before trial—"make the plaintiff attorney work for his money." Others will fight every case down to the bitter end— "make us a hard target for attorneys." The latter adopt the proposition that a plaintiff attorney burdened with too many cases, as the top money-winning liability attorneys are, will assign the harder targets less priority or settle out faster. The firm's officers naturally claim that this tactic has reduced the volume of claims they suffer, but there is no available evidence or even consensus of opinion on this point. The increase in legal costs occasioned by this philosophy may be borne by the firm under general counsel funding or spread to the insurance carrier in an agreed-upon, shared manner.

---

* In 1971, this figure was considered a claim under $2,000 or high claims that could be "bought off" for several thousand dollars. In a 1973 article,[8] Eginton presented a table of nine product cases that we might label nuisance and buy-off claims. These cases were defended by one firm over two years. Altogether, the plaintiffs sought almost $3 million in damages; legal costs for defense were about $40,000; and disposition (settlement) of the cases amounted to only $43,000.

The policy parameters become known throughout the organization: Service and rectification of complaints are affected accordingly. Through the legal grapevine, plaintiff attorneys receive word of which firms are "good" and which are "bad" targets. (Note that a "bad" target may find that a plaintiff attorney takes it on as a challenge, hoping to score a prestigious win and crack a tough opponent.) Product liability attorneys may have their clerks study court calendars for upcoming cases, or telephone all their friends handling similar cases, or find other means for helping one another. The firm then faces not a multitude of divided claims, but rather a series of claims that are each bolstered by a heavy exchange of engineering and legal information.

THE DEFENSE ATTORNEY

We have already discussed some of the preliminaries that the plaintiff and the defendant cover—the complaint, the bill of particulars, the interrogatories—so here we need look only at the guiding philosophies behind defending counsel's actions. In some firms, in-house counsel takes over the case and, in turn, works with the insurance firm's attorney. In others, particularly in small businesses, the complaint will go straight to the insurance company for complete handling through its chosen attorneys. In still others, in-house specialists or retained counsel will fight the case all the way. Warren Eginton, a noted defense attorney, claims that notification of the insurance carrier is not automatic or a matter of routine. The manufacturer, he says, is a self-insurer in certain claims; there might be some legal cost exemptions written into the policy to lower the premium rate. (The rate is also, of course, affected by the manufacturer's prior claim experiences.)

Generally, the insurer shoulders the legal defense costs, and while early settlement may mitigate them, they can never be entirely avoided once a suit has been entered against a firm. It is the insurer's obligation to defend a case completely regardless of the dollar limits of policy coverage. The insurer cannot "cut his losses" by paying off to the limits of the dollar coverage and presenting little or no defense when the plaintiff seeks more than this amount. The insurance firm's attorney must meet legally acceptable behavioral standards in the defense, seeking to mitigate the claim even though his fees are coming out of the insurer's pocket and he is working only to save the defendant firm's money.

As an example of how this might work: Consider a policy coverage limited to $500,000. Damage or injuries easily worth double that are sustained by a product user. The insurance company cannot pay off its policy and "walk away" from the case with a purely token defense. In a case where this happened and the award as expected was double the insurance coverage, the defendant company instituted a suit against its insurer for "throwing the case away." The defendant company won, and the insurance company had to foot the entire damage award plus all court costs.

Defense counsel is the person who discovers and tries the case. (The term "discovery" includes interrogatories, depositions, research, etc.) If counsel works as a team where one person (or more) does discovery and another takes this work product for preparation and presentation to the jury, the latter may be the litigator and the former in charge of the case. In other situations, the litigator himself will be in charge of the case with the person doing discovery subordinate to him. This in no way reflects on the caliber of the personnel involved; rather, it is a way of solving a timing problem. Litigators are bound by court calendars and tie their work to them, whereas discovery attorneys have a freer schedule and can accommodate themselves to the availability of company personnel, records, and so on. In a well-run office, the litigator is kept abreast of major developments in a case even if he or she is subordinate to another attorney. However, when the case starts moving to trial, the litigator takes the completed work and, in effect, assumes complete authority.

The choice of a defending attorney becomes particularly important in those states where the courts hold to the doctrine of strict liability. For example, the decision in a California case stated that "a manufacturer is strictly liable in tort when an article he places on the market, knowing that it is to be used without inspection for defects, proves to have a defect that causes injury to a human being." [9] As we emphasized earlier, if a defect in the product can be demonstrated, the manufacturer's liability extends beyond anything spelled out in warranties, "even if he committed no negligent act or omission and even if the person harmed had not purchased the product at all." [10]

The choice of attorney is crucial because such cases are hard to try and even harder to win.* Once the plaintiff proves that a fault existed in the product, through his engineer's examination or through application of *res ipsa*, the burden of proof shifts to the defense. It may try to demonstrate that misuse and abuse alone could have caused the defect. Or the defense may admit the existence of a defect but turn around and claim that such a defect presented no unreasonable combination of hazard and risk—no danger—until misuse and abuse on the part of the plaintiff converted the defect into an injury situation.

Two separate tire cases illustrate these defenses. In both cases it was alleged that broken bead wires caused accidents. The plaintiffs claimed strict liability. In the first case the defendant demonstrated how improper use of tools during the mounting of tires on wheels could break bead wires. The jury let the tire builder off the hook. In the second case, the tire had blown off the rim as it was being mounted, when the bead "let go." Here, the tire company accepted the charge of a defect in the bead. But it also proved that the plaintiff, by using an unregulated air filling hose, had overpressurized the tire to such an extent that when it did blow the damage done could properly be attributed to his action. Again, the tire builder was not liable. In both cases, one should note, it was the defense attorney who shouldered the burden of proof. The attorneys owed their success to intensive preparation, in which they directed their engineers to obtain what they needed and elicited their suggestions in depth.

---

* However, as we pointed out in Chapter 2, the plaintiff attorney is not assured of an automatic win. Even though the judge may charge the jury to rule on the basis of strict liability, many juries dislike the theory and rule accordingly.

Who should choose or review the choice of counsel? If the defendant's insurer is assigning someone to try the case, an in-house counsel should investigate the person chosen. If the defendant is using retained counsel, the in-house counsel should choose from a list of partners and associates supplied by the retained counsel's firm. It is not difficult to obtain an appraisal of a person's specialties and abilities in the legal field. If the trial attorney is a stock and bond specialist, the defendant need not retain him or otherwise compensate the retained counsel's firm for its personnel skill shortages. Also, the defendant's engineers should have an opportunity to talk with the potential defense counsel: This enables them to make a crucial evaluation of counsel's ability to learn the technical details they will feed him. If he does not appear to be able to do so, the engineers will advise their firm to find itself another attorney. In most firms such engineering review of attorney choice is totally unheard of—to the firms' detriment.

THE ATTORNEY'S ANALYSIS

The defense attorney knows full well that clinkers get through even the best production lines, that mistakes will be made in labeling, and that a bizarre set of circumstances can convert a harmless product into an accident producer. But his initial concern centers around whether the defect was one of design, in which every product of the type can be condemned, or whether there was an individual defect—the product design was good, but a casting or a component or the assembly was poor. Obviously design defects are much more serious, because a plaintiff victory in one case may trigger numerous similar suits, each citing a previous case as legal precedent.

Some defense attorneys use an interesting rule of thumb about what is a design defect: It is any defect which is not obvious and can cause injury. It can be likened to a trap. Open and notorious conditions are not design defects. Conditions that create a hazard but are necessary to the functioning of the device are not design defects. Examples of the latter are a welding torch, a meat grinder with an open top, and an onion-topping machine.

Certain products have a minimal safety standard built in; this standard is the measured risk the user takes. Such products cannot function with a greater safety margin. A prime example of this is an aircraft, which may have a 4:1 safety margin. That is, the bare minimum strength requirement is multiplied by four and this is considered sufficient; lift requirements put severe limits on allowable weight. The completely safe aircraft is unflyable.

If no design defect exists, the individual product may have a latent (or hidden) defect that arose during casting or molding. There still exist technological problems, for example, in controlling the melting processes of metals. While testing methods are important, one can test and retest a metal and still end up with a chain of nonmetallic inclusions or other flaws which will cause the product to fail.

The law applied to such cases differs from state to state. In some courts, even if the product was made with the greatest care, the fact that the defect was not discoverable is not a defense and the manufacturer is liable. In other states, the courts have held that the manufacturer does not have to make the perfect machine. The outcome of such a case hinges on the manufacturer's ability to prove that he operated to the extent of the state of the art and to demonstrate that he took all possible actions to maintain the highest-quality metals. If he proves this, the jury will be asked to find against the plaintiff on the grounds that the user assumes some risk in using any product: perfection is unattainable.

The defense counsel next determines the allowable cost of the defense. This cost is dictated largely by the seriousness of the injury, since the injury determines the range of possible verdicts against the defendant. Even if the defense counsel and the defendant personnel feel that the chance of a verdict against them is minimal, if the case involves loss of limbs or blinding or severe commercial damage, the defense budget is set at a high figure. Most attorneys are not given dollar figures as limits to their expenditures, but rather exercise common sense (from both business and legal viewpoints) in gauging their spending patterns. One large expenditure may be a visit to the plant or place of business of the defendant. With a local plant this is no financial burden. But when the distance is large, the question definitely is posed: Can a reasonable defense cost sustain such a trip? In firms where "fight every case" is the rule, the budget per case is kept lower and counsel are usually discouraged from traveling in order to keep costs down. Some insurance carriers frown on "junketing," but the major carriers and the foreign giants (such as Lloyds of London) give attorneys wide discretion.

Throughout the case, the defense attorney must work closely with defendant-firm personnel. Defense counsel meets first with top management people and discusses all facets of the suit: what the plaintiff claims happened, what damages are being sought, and so on. Then, with the aid of an organization chart, the attorney initiates a series of meetings with plant and department managers (design, production, quality control, and any others deemed advisable). Often all of this is shepherded by the defendant firm's newly appointed "product safety director." One of the worst things a firm can do is to appoint somebody's relative or golfing partner as the new "Vice President—Product Safety" to cover up previous omissions. The plaintiff attorney will investigate this new appointee and tear him apart in front of the jury. "This," he will point out, "is what the defendant firm thinks of product safety, when they appoint a man with such few credentials and at such a late date to run the product safety program."

Richard Markus, a prominent trial attorney, sees business as operating with three tiers of knowledge: [11] The high level is concerned with policy and overall considerations in operating the business and knows very little about how this policy is carried out. The middle level puts some of the policies into effect and leaves some of them out. The lower, functionary level does the work. Like the middle level, it does some of the things it is supposed to do and leaves out others. When the defense attorney examines a firm's operations, a comparison of overall policies, the way they are executed, and the firm's actual performance yields contrast and contradiction. Business researchers describe such distortions in terms of the top level setting goals, the middle level amplifying only the goals it likes, and the lower level displacing the goals so that feasibility matches the paper target.

The defense attorney, in this context, is more of a management diagnostician than legal counsel. If attorneys and company personnel are meeting each other for the first time, then much mutual familiarization must take place. If, on the other hand, they are long-time working partners on a multitude of cases, the specifics can be approached very quickly. In this regard, paradoxically, the firm with many cases pending against it may be better served than the one which has a rare occurrence. The latter type of firm should try to establish a working relationship with a good attorney who can handle upcoming product liability cases and who will familiarize himself with the workings of the firm so as to handle other legal business.

It is, unequivocally, the *defendant company's* ultimate responsibility to see to it that the person trying its case knows as much about the product—good, bad, and indifferent points—as anyone and everyone else connected with the product's conception, construction, and delivery. The attorney must be led by the hand through every phase of the product's design, manufacturing, testing, labeling, shipping, and sales. He or she must see the labels, the user instructions, the advertising, the sales training guides and classes, and all other material possible— whether pertinent or not. (Let the attorney make the judgment!) It is particularly important to point out to the attorney every file the company owns that is even remotely related to the product or class of products. The attorney should also be given every aid, secretarial and engineering, in obtaining and interpreting information.

In addition to delving into the physical and managerial-policy aspects of the firm, the attorney should be encouraged to develop his own perception of his client's overall approach to hazard elimination and risk reduction, and to communicate that perception to the defendant firm. In the preceding chapter we suggested that a manager use an interrogatory checklist as an offbeat audit of his firm's product safety efforts. Such an audit would prevent the all-too-common unpleasant surprise of having retained counsel arrive on the scene and destroy a facade of existing programs and efforts as he questions his own clients during case preparation. (Of course, better he should do it than the plaintiff attorney in court, as defenses can be prepared.)

The attorney should be given a complete product history and analysis, from physical creation to the product's condition when it leaves the shipping room dock. This includes all documentation that appears throughout the firm. The manager who hides failure reports from counsel will have a terrible time explaining why he did so when those records come out during a plaintiff's discovery proceeding. Similarly, it is not a bad thing for a manager showing counsel his department to reveal what he knows about shortcuts and shortcomings, deviations from the "book," and substitutions and changes that have not been documented. He should also supply complete test reports. There are firms which purge or sanitize their production records and "fool" counsel into believing this is the whole story. If the company does deceive counsel, it still must worry about the opposition. Any intelligent plaintiff attorney will immediately suspect that purging and sanitizing have taken place when he conducts his discovery, and will demand to see "all the records." When the company claims that remaining records are all that are available, the plaintiff attorney will attempt to get at least someone in the firm to admit in cross-examination that a record or part of a record was removed before the attorneys began combing the premises. The plaintiff attorney will demand to see that record. It is well to quote one of the rules of evidence: [12]

> Withholding or failing to produce evidence (documentary or real) which is available to a party and which he would ordinarily be expected to produce, may give rise to a presumption that the evidence was held back because it would be unfavorable. The strongest inferences may be drawn against the party who does so . . . .

The rule has been variously interpreted in different states to a greater or lesser degree of stringency. In some, it applies only to testimony: If a man is available to testify and is prevented by the firm from so doing, failure to produce him leads to a presumption that his testimony would be unfavorable.

Defense counsel should be encouraged to query any manufacturing, sales, or other personnel who may be able to enlighten him on any aspect of the product's genealogy or production. If counsel does not know enough to ask intelligent questions, manufacturing personnel should take all pains to bring him to a state of knowledge where he can ask probing questions. If a claimant's case appears to be a fair one, defense counsel will serve his client by playing devil's advocate—showing the firm where it was at fault and finding ways to save expenses through rapid settlement out of court.

All the while that this familiarization is going on, defense counsel will take extensive notes on what he sees and hears about the production process and the company's responses to plaintiff allegations about product shortcomings. These notes should be transcribed immediately and corrected by the appropriate personnel in the defendant firm, so that the case files hold specific, detailed memorandums on the entire proceedings that have taken place.

Eginton feels the first priority of the defense team is preservation.[13] He advises defense counsel to review and preserve the files, interrogate the witnesses (in the manner of a formal deposition), and, if possible, examine the actual product involved in the failure. Other attorneys suggest that if the product itself is not available, samples of the same type of product, built at the same time and in the same production run, should be obtained and preserved—even if this means inducing a customer to accept a swap for a newer and later model at no cost.

The defense should make every attempt to gain access to the faulty product, either before, coincident with, or after the above process of familiarization. The plaintiff will be very reluctant to let the product out of his possession, and the defendant may have to obtain a court order of discovery to gain access to it. The plaintiff's expert may have to be present at the product's examination, particularly if there is a possibility the defendant might change something during his tests.

Assuming that possession of the product is gained, the first step for the defendant is to identify it as his. Exploded grinding wheels, for example, bear no identification; more than one firm has cranked up for a full defense and then had composition tests by a chemistry laboratory prove "it's not our wheel." Moral: It may have been bought in your box, but you may have had no hand in putting it there. Incidentally, if you do sell surplus boxes with your name on them for someone else's use, don't trust him to delete same. He may push your name with an inferior product; your selling him the boxes contributed to misleading the customer, which can only lead to your own corporate headache.

As mentioned earlier, a firm may sometimes become involved in a failure fault of two or more manufacturers without knowing it. In Chapter 2 we discussed and illustrated the damage to an electric range heating element and griddle. Suppose one of the flying metallic particles had actually injured the homemaker's eye and each manufacturer had been sued separately. The heating element alone makes an impressive court exhibit; the gaping hole at point A (Figure 1) is grist for a *res ipsa loquitur* case, and the deterioration at point B may include warranty as well as negligence aspects. The physician who treated the eye is very unlikely to have saved the particle that was removed, and if it did not come from the element, the defendant would have no way of knowing that fact. The firm might consent to a large settlement to cut its costs for defense and preparation.

At the same time, the plaintiff attorney might negotiate separately with the griddle manufacturer. Figures 2 and 3, showing the damaged griddle, are also impressive. The company might never suspect an allied failure could have contributed to this result. No metallurgist can deny that some bizarre metallic defect could have been present in the casting and caused it to explode into thousands of tiny particles. Again, the plaintiff has a *res ipsa* negligence and even possible warranty case—and a possible settlement without preparation.

To prevent this situation from developing, with two or more firms settling in ignorance, it is necessary that defendant firms do prepare a defense and do learn of other parties being sued. The mechanisms to use include interrogatories and depositions, as will be discussed later in this chapter. The two firms may join in one equitable settlement, possibly shared in some equitable ratio.

Next, the product should be traced by serial number, or model number, through the entire production process. The objective here is to connect the defect on hand with a point in time (or place at which) said defect might have occurred. It might have occurred when parts were still with a vendor and not yet delivered to the manufacturer. Or the damage to the product may have been unlikely anywhere else but in the distribution network beyond the manufacturer's door. The defendant experts should, at the very least, cover the same conceptual outline of design, construction, test, inspection, and warning used for the plaintiff's expert witness. Armed with superior knowledge of the product and test facilities, it is incumbent upon the firm to perform all the tests it can to discover just where the defect was generated and, if it occurred in the plant, how it got past inspection.

Some problems occur right in the retail dealer's store. The dealer may purchase bicycles in boxes and assemble them carelessly, leading to faulty brake operation. Should an accident occur, the manufacturer can, with due care in preparation of its case, pin the blame where it rightfully belongs. Commercial fertilizer sold in drums may be repackaged and improperly marked by a small dealer. If the dealer was warned about proper marketing and failed to follow through, the firm can pin the blame on him no matter how hard the plaintiff attorney tries to get the "big fish" with the deeper pocket.

Some defense attorneys feel very strongly that the product should be sent to an independent certifying laboratory or expert for an official report instead of to the office or plant where it was constructed. The defense seeks to establish that it has used a neutral independent witness and makes great store of this at the trial. Again, we have the problem of partisanship: The independent witness who consistently tells his corporate clients that they were at fault, and finds no "socially redeeming value" to defend, soon finds he has no corporate clients. If the witness's report is made available to the plaintiff by court order, and it usually is, the defendant won't want the report to supply fresh ammunition to the enemy. The telephone becomes a major reporting medium for serious defects uncovered, with written reports kept bland to the point of uselessness to the plaintiff. The end result can be a report which carefully skirts attributable blame characteristics and focuses on what is right with the product.

Some experts who make court appearances and do liability work regularly are very "professional" in turning out the most bland and unrevealing reports. Frequently they confine themselves to extensive descriptions of the product as received by them, loads of photographs, unkind comments about how plaintiff's expert chopped up the product, and unequivocal statements that there was no defect in the product as seen by them.

In the preceding chapter we mentioned that the plaintiff engineer sometimes has to chop the product apart in his examination. He turns over to the defendants something that looks more like a box of scrap than a device. Hence, defendant engineers go out of their way to take photographs and write complete descriptions of what they receive as a form of self-protection against accusations that they changed something to confuse the jury in the follow-on trial. This is particularly true if the plaintiff engineer was not present when the product was delivered to the company.

When the product is such a box of scrap, the defendant engineers try very hard, through their attorneys, to get the plaintiff engineer's report. Since the plaintiff attorney expects such a request, and will probably honor it, he may well have asked at the very first meeting with his expert for a bland report, again with major details kept verbal. Defendant engineers then direct their attorney in propounding questions for the interrogatories or depositions. Looking at the "scrap," listening to the responses or reading transcripts of depositions, and working with the full facilities of the firm, the defendant's engineers can often put together a pretty good reconstruction of the events leading to the accident.

Which brings us back to the discussion of interrogatories, depositions, and discovery. From the defendant's point of view, these should be used to open up the plaintiff's entire case. Let's examine how they can be used to help the defendant through the posing of who, what, when, where, and why questions.

Interrogatories should be used to find out exactly *who* the plaintiff is using as an engineer. This name should be completely investigated by the company librarian, especially if the person's credentials include publications or memberships in professional societies. Most professional societies have minimal membership requirements—sometimes only a degree in the sciences. The key to establishing true competence is not simply membership, but activity on specific committees dealing, for example, with standards applicable to the defendant company's products. The degree to which the engineer serves as a far-ranging professional litigation witness may be useful knowledge if his credibility is to be impeached or if his performance under pressure is to be gauged. Some witnesses appear in courts on a regular basis and earn a major part of their income by claiming expertise in everything from gas dynamics to home appliances. Their success is rooted in their ability to play a convincing role before the jury and capitalize on the defendant's lack of research into the true nature of their expertise.

Interrogatories should also tell the defense attorney who else is involved in the accident—such as which retailer, distributor, other manufacturer charged with a fault in the incident, witnesses to the before- and after-accident effects (particularly where consequential damages or permanent disability is being claimed), and anyone else who may have knowledge of the situation. In particular, the defense attorney should find out if more than one plaintiff engineer examined the product. There may have been three investigations, with the first two engineers reporting no negligence and the third giving a report leading to the suit. Defense counsel might try to find out why the first two opinions were rejected.

"What" questions attempt to find out exactly what are the weaknesses in the plaintiff's case. The plaintiff engineer may be testifying on tire construction but may have had no exposure to tire manufacturing processes. He may be basing his knowledge on trade sources and outdated materials not recognized as authoritative in the field. His tests, due to financial or facility limitations, may have missed the central issue of the case or even yielded erroneous data. All this can be used to impeach his credibility in front of the jury. It is extremely important, therefore, for defendant engineers to help the defense counsel go over every statement and characteristic introduced by the plaintiff, from the bill of particulars through the ultimate courtroom testimony.

A useful trick sometimes employed by researchers is that of "matched pages." Here, each page in a transcript of testimony or a deposition is laborously matched against all preceding pages, one after another. This means scanning material over and over again as one gets deeper into the transcript. But it is rare that such an examination lets a weakness or damaging contradiction slip by. In one case it gradually dawned on an engineer that his adversary expert witness had made several statements incorrectly quoting a reference text. The expert's knowledge of the text became suspect, and sure enough, at the trial the defense counsel effectively destroyed his impact by showing up his errors. When two or three people are reviewing a set of transcripts, they should first go over them separately, making marginal notes where appropriate. Then one of them should be appointed a reader: He or she reads the transcripts line by line until coming to an item of substance—a marginal note that calls for discussion. The others then refer to the transcripts and other documents to find statements on that matter. Contradictions, changes, and omissions should be carefully noted.

The "when" of the plaintiff's case is also very important. Recall that the statute of limitations starts from the date of the accident. Some plaintiff attorneys practice brinkmanship and, hoping to settle without trial, will not enter court action until shortly before the statute runs out. Such delays sometimes indicate the degree of sincerity with which the attorney has been prosecuting the case.

"When" is also important from the standpoint of indicating how late in the case the expert witness was brought on the scene. Expenditures for an expert can be costly and sometimes are not made until the last minute, when the plaintiff sees how weak his case is without one. If local conditions contributed to the accident or its severity, defendant engineers should be prepared, if possible, to show how conditions may have changed between the date of the accident and the date of the engineer's investigation. It is important to point out here that if a defendant makes repairs, changes, or improvements to his products after an accident, such actions cannot be brought up in court or used against him in any way to prove that something had been wrong in the first place. The repairs, changes, or improvements are after the fact of the accident and may not be mentioned in court. For example, a defective tire-production line which produces broken beads can be changed without that being construed in any way as a mark against the defendant. In this case, the higher good of society is served by not discouraging the defendant from making continuous repairs and improvements.

"Where" questions pertain chiefly to the jurisdiction in which the accident took place and where the case will be tried. An accident in Miami may be tried in New York (federal court) if that is the location of the defendant's home office.

Some defense attorneys use "where" questions to trace the movement of evidence from expert to expert, if more than one was involved, and to trace the product backwards to the date of distribution by the firm to see if it might have been abused in some way along the stream of commerce. Also, "Where is the evidence now?" may be extremely important if it was contaminated food or some other perishable product; continued proper storage is necessary if investigations are to be fruitful and reveal at least a modicum of what was present at the time of the alleged accident. In a surprisingly large number of instances, the evidence simply vanishes before the defendant can get a look at it. While the judge may dismiss the case out of hand (no evidence, no case), usually the plaintiff does not suffer nearly as much as the defendant would in a similar situation. In an electrical explosion case, a huge panel-mounted circuit breaker "vanished in the smoke." The plaintiff attorney actually had the jury convinced that it had disintegrated in the explosion. The defendant did not have the presence of mind to bring a sample into the courtroom—a 600-ampere insulated copper box measuring approximately $30'' \times 10'' \times 6''$ and weighing about 50 pounds—and suffered in the verdict.

"Why" questions trace the causality of the accident and, most important, all the events that led up to it. Industrial accidents, for example, are frequently "telegraphed" to careful observers. That is, a manufacturer's service representative, field liaison, or sales representative will sometimes report back that he or she saw "an accident waiting to happen" in a customer's plant. A safety device may have been short-circuited or bad operational practices may have been commonplace in the plant—with the representative's warning to plant management falling on deaf ears.

By the same token, consumer product accidents may also have been telegraphed by a succession of complaints or returns. Some part of the product may show an alarming frequency of breaks or may cause frequent breakdown of adjacent components. The alert manager, in either the industrial or the consumer situation, will be on the lookout for the messages he is getting and investigate the matter in order to prevent, where possible, the ultimate injury-producing event.

The company in which managers are *not* alert will overlook these messages—and the plaintiff attorney will point this out to the jury if he discovers it. The plaintiff attorney will play down the responsibility of the industrial customer who, say, wired a safety switch closed. He may even use the fact that it was seen and not objected to by the manufacturer as indicating the latter's tacit approval. In the consumer product situation, the plaintiff attorney will point out to the jury that the company was on notice that there was a problem situation and claim that this indeed proves the company was more interested in making money than in protecting the users of its products. Thus, asking "why" questions helps the defense attorney anticipate the plaintiff's case and to prepare his defenses accordingly.

In our discussion of the law, we pointed out that a statement of fact or an action by a firm's representative can give rise to an extension of that firm's express warranty. It therefore becomes extremely important to find out why the customer bought the product, why he used it as he did, and why (if applicable) he thought it would withstand the abuse he gave it. Defense counsel may discover that a company salesman claimed things and degrees of safety that the people in the design department see as goals ten years hence. That salesman may have acted in good faith, but his mistake is a breach of warranty when something goes wrong. Salesmen will also have read their company's patent announcements. In an attempt to provide a comprehensive description of the patent, a firm's attorneys and engineers may indeed have been futuristic in thinking about the capabilities and safety of the product. These documents are, of course, available to the plaintiff and he will obtain them from the patent office, especially when breach of warranty offers an avenue for litigation.

Our brief summary of investigative questions leads us now to the subject of handling interrogatories and depositions initiated by the plaintiff. Defendant's retained counsel will usually provide the client with specific instructions, but what many law firms do is turn over the interrogatory to the client firm's risk manager for a "first cut" at answering the questions. The risk manager (or quality control chief or chief engineer) will round up the talent necessary to provide the initial draft of a response. Counsel will then take the role of devil's advocate with each person involved and do the necessary editing. Interrogatories yield slowly formulated and deliberate answers.

Depositions, on the other hand, are much like trial testimony in the precautions one should observe when answering. We cover this in the next chapter, but several caveats are in order here. First, a deposition, although taken under oath and recorded, is not like a trial in that when a witness's attorney objects and is sustained by the judge at a trial, the witness may then be allowed to refuse to answer. In a deposition a witness must, in most jurisdictions, answer all the questions put to him. The attorney objects during a deposition so that later there is a possibility of preventing the material from being heard by the jury in the courtroom, but the deposition witness must still answer the question. If an attorney fails to object at the deposition the judge at the later trial may not accept an objection in court to the same question; the witness's statement at the deposition will be read back to him—to his possible detriment. In practice, this "object," "answer the question" sequence can create considerable confusion in the minds of defendant managers and engineers. Before the deposition they may be carefully prepared to stay away from certain areas of operations and reveal nothing. When the sensitive questions start coming during the deposition, the manager or engineer may become evasive or, worse, lose his composure. He expects his attorney to object and cut off the line of questioning. Instead, the attorney objects and then directs him to answer to what a few minutes before he was ordered to stay away from. Knowledge of the procedure involved should help the witness in this situation.

The range of questions asked during the deposition may be far wider than would be true at the trial. And once a witness has revealed sensitive information and weaknesses, no amount of objections will erase the facts from the adversary's mind. Defense witnesses are advised to answer the questions in a short, sweet, and to-the-point manner; to volunteer nothing; to be careful to listen to the entire question before answering; and to worry about the questions one at a time. The plaintiff attorney is looking for spontaneous answers that will expose weaknesses. Interrupting him, or talking too much, or trying to correct prior answers will serve only to accomplish his purpose. A good preparation session with the defense attorney should clear up any other problems.

The defense attorney will also be posing interrogatories and conducting depositions of the plaintiff side. Quite often the defense attorney will have his engineer sit in on a deposition-taking, particularly when the plaintiff's expert witness is under examination. There are both advantages and disadvantages to having the engineer present. The advantages are that the defendant engineer can gauge his opponent's technical capability, he can help formulate lines of attack on freshly exposed weaknesses, he can pick up details of information his attorney might miss, and he gets a gut feeling for the overall strength of the plaintiff's attack. During the course of a deposition it may become obvious that the plaintiff's case has many technical weaknesses (in the engineering sense). In such situations, defense counsel may deliberately refrain from probing too deeply and exposing many of the plaintiff's weaknesses, with a view toward exposing them instead at the trial. (Why help your enemy map his own terrain?) Alternatively, the probing may be relentless and the expert witness may be forced into admitting a lack of knowledge on many technical points. This testimony can be used against him later on at a trial.

There are several disadvantages to having the defendant's engineer present at the deposition of the plaintiff's expert witness. For one thing, the defense attorney becomes "lazy"; instead of deeply immersing himself in all the details of the case so that he can pick and probe at every response, he uses his own expert as a crutch. Frequent whispered conversations and asides break thought patterns and have the same effect as a commercial during a TV drama. The defendant engineer doesn't want to be too obtrusive and usually waits for his attorney to turn to him—so valuable lines of questioning often go unchecked. Many expert witnesses agree that in depositions where the opposition has an attending engineer as a crutch, the attorney tends to prepare less well and also displays less of the "shot of adrenalin" that should be visible when he discovers a weakness.

The defense builds a file of documents that will show, in court, how the product was designed, built, tested, and so forth. The following is only a partial list of the types of documents that can accomplish this:

Machine genealogy
Correspondence with customers
Competitors' experiences with like products
Other customers' experiences with product
Blueprints and schematics
Rejection and acceptance reports
Reject history
Quality control procedures and checklists
Quality control manuals

Actions taken on suggestions for reducing defects

Inspection and test reports

Laboratory test reports

Compliance reports re government regulations

Compliance reports re industry standards and customs

Compliance with standards of professional organizations

Sales literature

Sales slip showing warranty

Checklists covering inclusion of instruction manuals in shipments

Field failure manuals

Feedback from salesmen

Feedback from service organizations

Past liability claims

Statements from witnesses

Photos before and after

All other evidence that shows the firm is safety-conscious

All other information that may help prove the firm was not negligent and should not be held in strict liability

Defense counsel will need to "work and work and work" if he hopes to mitigate the claim. Even if it does look like a clinker got through the plant, in-depth defense preparation has threefold benefits: The defense's negotiating arm (to be discussed in the next chapter) is strengthened, the image of an inviting target is reduced, and the defendant is probably defended when he should be defended. Also, the net effect is often to wear down and overwhelm the plaintiff.

In the next chapter we detail the meeting of the plaintiff and defendant in court. Here we will explore the negotiating process which is carried on at all times, up to and including the very moment the jury is about to be sent out of the room for a verdict. A manager, in developing his business sense of how to prevent product liability, cannot be constantly in touch with his attorney, but he can learn to think of "how this will appear in court." If he is aware of the five areas in which the product may be attacked (design, construction, testing, inspection, warning) and of the fact that his actions in these areas will ultimately be judged before a jury, he should be able to develop a sense of liability prevention that is just as valid as his abilities in other business areas.

REFERENCES

1. The material in this section is largely reprinted from Irwin Gray's earlier paper "Consider the User: Management's Philosophies, Myopias, and Operations as They Affect the User of Its Products," *Proceedings PLP 70,* Newark, N.J. (August 26–28, 1970), pp. 97–98. Used by permission of the copyright holder, the American Society for Quality Control.
2. Jay W. Lorsch, *Product Innovation and Organization* (New York: Macmillan, 1965), p. 1.
3. Ibid., p. 27.
4. Ibid., p. 28.
5. Ibid., p. 30.
6. Thomas J. Watson, Jr., *A Business and Its Beliefs* (New York: McGraw-Hill, 1963), p. 31.
7. Theodore V. Houser, *Big Business and Human Values* (New York: McGraw-Hill, 1957), p. 38.
8. Warren W. Eginton, "Minimizing Product Liability Exposure," *Quality Progress* (January 1973), p. 22.
9. Greenman v. Yuba Power Products Inc., 59 Cal. 2d 57, 377 P. 2d 897, 27 Cal. Rptr. 697 (1963).
10. *Products Liability: Minimizing the Hazard* (New York: Commerce Clearing House, 1971), p. 5.
11. Richard M. Markus, "The Discovery Tools." *ATL Counseling Cassettes,* Vol. 4, No. 2, Association of Trial Lawyers of America, 1974.
12. Hon. Eugene R. Canudo, *Evidence Laws of New York* (New York: Gould Publications, 1971), p. 17.
13. Eginton, op. cit., p. 24.

4

THE TRIAL

A trial is not a dispassionate and cooperative effort by all the parties to arrive at justice. It is the adversary system, the competitive system in the administration of law. In a court there is a judge who is to pass on the questions, and there are lawyers on each side. . . . But neither the judge nor any other representative of the public is active in developing the facts. The lawyers are the ones who develop and present the case. They do so, each for his own side and not for both sides. If one lawyer is poor or lazy, his side suffers accordingly. If the other lawyer is unscrupulous, his side may benefit unduly.[1]

—M. M. CHEATHAM

At the close of a seminar on product liability prevention, a question was posed by the manager of a foundry. The seminar had stressed the point that all records should be retained as long as possible. The manager was distraught: His firm runs chart recorders for every heat, resulting in graphic records that are each about 100 feet long and 6 inches wide. Even tightly rolled these present a monumental storage problem; the firm had been taking tabular, one-page analyses off the records and storing these. The graphs were discarded after six months. Now, however, the foundry manager was forced to ask: How would it look in court if the plaintiff attorney attacked the short analyses and pointed an accusing finger at a firm which "discarded its original records"?

There is no definitive answer to this question. However, if the plaintiff attorney did try this tactic, is there not an effective counterploy that would yield a fine defense? Assume the plaintiff attorney hammers at the point that the company should have kept an original record—and was hiding something by not having done so. At the first opportunity defense counsel should have two people unroll a typical chart—preferably one that resembles the missing one. It is very impressive to a jury as two people walk away from each other and unwind a 100-foot strip of paper. For the defense: "Reasonable persons in the jury should be able to see that storage of these things represents a monumental problem the company has surmounted with its one-page analysis sheets."

The manager who keeps in mind "How will this look to the jury?" has an excellent decision framework for liability prevention. It is the same framework the plaintiff and defense attorneys use to guide their own actions—only the manager seeks prevention, while the attorneys are adversaries. In this chapter we move from the preparation stage into and through the court system, where the adversaries meet to resolve opposing viewpoints.

SETTLEMENT TRIES

The courtroom is not the first place where the two adversaries meet. Aside from depositions, discovery activities, and other communications, a very serious negotiating "game" has been going on to settle the case before going to trial. Karrass states that "a negotiation takes place whenever ideas are exchanged for the purpose of influencing behavior." [2] Negotiation is a bargaining process within the rules of the law for very high stakes.

We know from negotiation experiments run by Karrass [3] and confirmed by experienced trial lawyers that large initial demands improve the chances of winning. The plaintiff attorney always starts with a huge figure when he feels he has a good case, in order to wage a war of nerves against the other side and also to guard against winning an eventual court battle in which he asked and received too little. Skilled negotiators aiming at high settlements are often able to bring about larger awards for the plaintiff (even when their cases are weak) than negotiators who are more modest in their demands.

A plaintiff's case is immeasurably strengthened if he retains an important, big-name trial attorney who personally conducts the settlement negotiations as opposed to having an associate doing so. Insurance companies anticipate higher jury verdicts with name attorneys and settle accordingly. They recognize that the more skilled the plaintiff attorney, the more he will win in his settlement, even if he and his opponent had cases of equal strength.[4]

The defendant attorney wants to buy off a case as cheaply as possible—"his nightmare is that he might give a figure higher than that which plaintiff lawyer would have accepted."[5] As noted above, the plaintiff attorney starts at an astronomical figure. He then constantly changes his negotiating position so that he shows first one strong point and then another as he forces the other side up and up in its offers.

Nizer tells us that many insurance companies find plaintiff attorneys coming to trial unprepared.[6] This is indirectly confirmed by Supreme Court Chief Justice Warren Burger, who has stated that in his experience as a lawyer and a judge, between one-third and one-half of the nation's trial lawyers are insufficiently trained.[7] When insurers see that the plaintiff attorney is poorly prepared, they conclude that he probably never intends to go to trial and wants to settle out of court as quickly as possible. Instead of making an offer, they put time pressure on him by dragging things out interminably. When he asks for an offer, they respond by asking him how much *he* thinks the case is worth as a "reasonable man." By stretching negotiations over a long period of time and constantly getting the plaintiff to reduce his settlement figure, they effectively get him to bid against himself until they have a sacrificial settlement on their records. When the case finally reaches trial, they can proceed to final negotiations and demand further reductions in the interest of compromise.[8]

Even during the trial the process of reaching a settlement by negotiation will go on—to the very moment before the jury announces its verdict. Negotiation takes place behind the scenes— in the attorneys' offices, in the hallway outside the courtroom, and even in judges' chambers. The whole process must never be revealed to the jury, because, as Nizer explains:

> . . . otherwise the jury might draw the inference that one party deemed himself negligent or that the other considered his case worth far less than he was demanding in court. Neither inference would be justified. The parties may be willing to make sacrifices to avoid litigation, but this should not prejudice their rights to a fair trial. Furthermore, as a practical matter, settlement discussions would be rare if the penalty for holding an unsuccessful one was that the jury would learn of the concessions which both parties were ready to make.[9]

Jeans has likened the settlement process to the negotiations for the sale of a product.[10] He lays down four basic principles in evaluating a claim:

1. The location of the trial to be.
2. The timing of the case.
3. The case salesmen.
4. The intrinsic worth of the "article."

The location (or venue) of a trial is very important because the law is applied in different ways in different states. Legal technicalities make it more difficult to prove certain points, or demonstrate evidence of negligence, in some states than in others. Furthermore, when the plaintiff goes into the discovery stage, well before trial, in some states he is more likely to be blocked by judges upholding a corporate refusal to supply some material (as irrelevant). A judge in a state dominated by giant, influential corporations may hesitate before allowing what the corporation will call "a plaintiff's aimless fishing expedition." In other states, the judge may encourage discovery of even the most peripheral matters and create no end of problems for the corporate defendant. The firm may even have to open up for discovery files and operations that are remote in location from the plant directly involved in the case—including those of corporate headquarters and entire divisions of the firm.

Location also bears directly on the type of juror to be expected. An attorney practicing in a semi-rural area had to work twice as hard on defense cases because, he said, "on entering a courtroom I would have to deal with farmer juries, a farmer plaintiff, and a judge who knew everyone. Against this stood a big, impersonal company who, everyone knew, was backstopped by a bigger, even more impersonal insurance firm." The major things which prevented justice from being twisted were the innate sense of fair play on the part of all concerned and the attorney's efforts to insure the presence of the local dealer (to reduce the "impersonal gap").

Both sides are also well attuned to the range of verdicts that juries bring in. Some insurance firms have excellent files cross-listing injury, age of victim, and location against jury awards; their value in guiding offer limits during negotiations is obvious. While such information is public—available in court records—few plaintiff attorneys have the resources to match that information bank.

Next, Jeans calls attention to the timing of the case. He likens the timing problem to the selling of Christmas trees after January First. Many, many cases are settled after the plaintiff puts his first expert on the stand—who, in a strong case, might make a devastating impact on the jury. On the other hand, the case may be settled because the expert "blows" the case through poor presentation or is torn apart in cross-examination. A case may be settled immediately after a jury is chosen, when one side or the other sizes up the people as unfavorable. Experienced attorneys try to estimate the jury settlement and the risks of losing versus a settlement "in hand" for a known amount.

Judges may call attorneys into their chambers and try to obtain a settlement before the jury is chosen. Some judges will press hard for a settlement even if the initial differences in demands are far apart; they cast an "evil eye" on the attorney who is not bending enough. Other judges will quite agreeably allow a six-figure case to go to trial with only a few hundred dollars difference between the attorneys' demands.

While both plaintiffs and defendants are heard to decry the long delays involved in moving a case to trial, the truth of the matter is that either side may benefit from such delays. Witnesses may become unavailable—they move to distant points, die, or just "disappear" and become untraceable. Depositions they gave earlier can be read into the record at the trial, but this is equivalent to reading a script versus seeing the play. Sometimes the plaintiff dies—his estate may continue the suit, but the value of the verdict obviously suffers. The plaintiff's case may be helped by a delay if formerly unknown medical sequelae develop into visible impairment, or if inflation increases the size of the potential settlement or verdict. The defendant may benefit if a court decision in a related case goes against the plaintiff, or if the plaintiff's injuries and impairment are ameliorated over time (as when a child "grows out" of his or her impairment or overcomes the effects of an injury). Various proposals have been put forward to foster faster settlements by forcing companies to pay interest on the award from date of suit. In some court jurisdictions this is already in effect, but there is no evidence that this has any beneficial effect in speeding claim settlements.[11]

Next is the question of the case salesmen: Who represents the plaintiff, and who represents the defendant? When big names square off, the game is played for much higher stakes. And while the jury may be ignorant of the reputations of the people facing them, they can quickly see that the performance they are watching is being played by stars. There is an aura, an ambience, if you will, of an operation run by big names—when they take an interest in the case—that cannot be matched by lesser lights. The caveat "when they take an interest in the case" is included because in some cases associates prepare a case poorly, the overloaded star picks it up on the weekend before, and all his expertise does not prevent disaster at the trial. In every attorney's office there are horrible examples of cases where it was discovered that an expert was needed for an engineering opinion—which the associates had not called for earlier—and the expert was sent into the courtroom on short notice. In such instances it is brought out in court that the expert came on the scene late and "has not been with the case long enough to learn it properly" —with the jury invited to make a "proper evaluation" of this.

Finally, evaluation of a claim must take into account the "intrinsic worth of the article." In many jurisdictions, cases are increasingly being tried in two parts. The first trial determines only liability: Is the defendant liable or not? If he is liable, a second trial with a completely new jury takes place and this second one determines the amount. Settlement can, of course, take place at any time in the process. But the attorneys evaluate the chance that the defendant will be held liable and the verdict range, and plug this into their expected-worth calculations for settlement. In the flower bed case described in an earlier chapter, liability is almost certain to be proved. The verdict range can likewise be determined, by assuming at one extreme that all the company's dire economics are true and by being somewhat less pessimistic at the other.

While these four items carry the greatest weight in settlement negotiations, a host of other considerations are operative as well. Some of these have been alluded to previously, including:

1. The history of how the firm treated the plaintiff before the suit was actually started.
2. Who the expert witness is and his track record of impressing juries.
3. How well an expert's report has been written.
4. How well company engineers and sales personnel come across under questioning.
5. How impressive the firm's product safety program is— or was it set up the week after the accident?
6. Who the plaintiff is—an earthy gardener showing his calloused hands to the jury or a more nondescript person.
7. Who the defendant is—a local dealer or a giant; a company with a bad reputation or a good one.
8. How badly pressed the plaintiff is for medical payments or a cash infusion to his business to repair accident damage.

PREPARING FOR THE TRIAL

With the failure of negotiations for settlement, the case moves toward resolution by a jury or (if both sides agree) by a judge.

The exact court date can never be exactly set in advance, and people involved in the trial are often deeply frustrated by the it's on–it's off–it's now–it's later scheduling of a trial. Consider for a moment that a trial involves:

A plaintiff attorney
A defendant attorney
Plaintiff experts and witnesses
Defendant experts and witnesses
The plaintiff
The defendant—or corporate representative
A courtroom
A jury
A judge
A continuous flow of cases preceding yours, none of whose duration can be exactly predetermined
Sickness, injury, and other unforeseen factors necessitating postponements.

The attorney must meet with his or her witnesses and carefully go over the depositions they gave (possibly some years before), review any problems they had at the depositions with sticky questions, and convey the need for proper attitude and appearance.[12] Not only are the answers important, but there must be no display of bias or prejudice inside, outside, or around the courtroom at any time. You never know who is watching or listening to your words. At the trial, the witness will be confronted with answers he gave on interrogatories and depositions, and seemingly irrelevant points will suddenly highlight contradictions or areas for the other side to zero in on. If time is available, the entire deposition should be reviewed by a thorough question-and-answer session. At this time the witness who is being prepared to testify should insist on telling his story and not allow the attorney to do all the talking.

The need for thorough preparation to ferret out any avenues of weakness may be discerned in the following case: An expert witness testified for a firm against a landlord who had allowed a freight elevator to remain unusable for six months. The plaintiff sought compensation for extra help and delays in moving merchandise up and down stairs. The expert had made time studies in which professionally recognized fatigue factors, rating factors, and other allowances were used to calculate how long it would take to move a truckload of merchandise out of the building to the loading platform. When the plaintiff attorney asked the expert to give his data during the trial, the judge took over the questioning and asked how long it had taken to load the truck from the raw times that had been clocked in the trial runs. The expert could not answer the question, as all calculations had been made with adjusted times. The judge said he wanted no "technical mumbo jumbo" and tore the witness apart in front of the jury. Scratch one case!

In a good preparation session, the attorney would have had the expert give his testimony with all the technical backup and then repeat same for the nontechnical people (the judge and jury).

Before the trial, the attorney should get all his witnesses together and go over with them his timing and how he plans to use their testimony. Group preparation of witnesses also allows an interchange of ideas and the clearing up or reconciliation of conflicts.[13] Some attorneys follow the practice of giving the witness a written outline of the questions he intends to ask—although this has obvious dangers.

The case moves to trial in either state or federal courts. The former has jurisdiction if plaintiff and defendant are from the same state, while the latter requires that the case possess "diversity of interests" (different states or countries) and be worth over $10,000.

From the moment the witness or anyone else connected with the case arrives at the courthouse, he is "on stage." [14] Dress is as important as the costuming for a major theatrical production. *The Wall Street Journal* tells of a six-figure-income attorney who typically arrives in court in a "baggy tweed jacket with elbow patches and badly frayed sleeves. One of his scuffed shoes is separating at the seam. He carries a battered briefcase." [15] He is, of course, trying to gain the sympathy of juries and aid the cause of his clients.

In a plaintiff's case, a man who had lost part of his eyesight came from Miami without glasses and, appropriate to the beach, in sports attire. Plaintiff attorneys intercepted him at the door and in a short time he returned in dark blue suit, white shirt, tie, and dark glasses. Unfair? Please reread the paragraph at the beginning of this chapter—our adversary system is in operation.

JURY SELECTION

In choosing a jury, both attorneys know what type of people they want. In state courts they are allowed to question the prospective jurors; in federal courts, the judge does the questioning.

Usually, both the defense and plaintiff attorneys try to keep technically trained people off accident-case juries. They don't want a technical specialist going into the jury room and becoming a self-appointed instructor to everyone else. The jury is supposed to make up its collective mind on the basis of what was seen and heard in the courtroom, not on the basis of a private, unchallenged tutorial by a technically trained juror.

Laing notes that the shrewd defense attorney will shun young jurors "because of do-gooder mentalities" and will look for "people able to resist the impulse to give the plaintiff the moon—retired people living on a fixed income and older blue collar and middle management workers. They are accustomed to shifting for themselves and are usually conservative in awards." [16] Laing further points out that some defense attorneys sow dissension in the jury by trying to exploit racial tension and class conflict in selections. A disunified jury rarely grants large awards.

Jury selection is a highly subjective art. The process of examining the qualifications and biases of a jury panel (the group of citizens called to serve, from which a jury is selected) is called voir dire. Some attorneys look at the process as a "weeding out." They can't select people—only reject them, within the limitations established by the court in question. The attorneys from both sides attempt to gauge how the various people on the jury panel will respond to the information they receive during the trial and whether they are likely to find for or against the plaintiff.

Some juries have twelve people, some nine, some eight, and

others six—again depending on the court jurisdiction. The verdict they render can be by anything from simple majority to unanimity. In a civil case, of the type we are discussing here, unanimity is generally not necessary: The verdict can be established by 10 jurors out of 12, 5 out of 6, or some other combination.

In most jurisdictions, by the way, there exist one or more jury-investigation services. Such services put out books of reports on people who are called for a panel. A book gives a complete background on the juror—his neighborhood, employment, race, some details about his family, religion, and political background, and his voting record in previous court trials. In some states a juror may be on a panel for only two weeks and hear only two or three cases, while in other states the service on a panel may be a month or longer and the juror hears enough cases to establish a lengthy voting record. Jury-investigation services will analyze every civil court trial in a particular jurisdiction, and their reports on the juror tell just how he (and the rest of the jury) found. The reports also discuss the cases involved, so that if a particular case matches the one at hand and there was a unanimous verdict, a juror's predilections may be foretold to some degree. Attorneys also speak to jurors after a trial and glean a great deal of information about them and their responses to what they saw in the courtroom. This information is also traded among attorneys.[17]

How important is careful selection? Very, according to a number of studies conducted at the University of Chicago.[18] Researchers found that on any given 12-person jury, the decisions will be made by three or four leaders and the rest of the group then follows. Picking out who these leaders are, questioning them closely, and using a book of reports is at least one way of assuring that the attorney does not start out at a disadvantage. Attorneys quickly become experts on psychology, group dynamics, body language, and the interpretation of personality manifestations.

A note of advice to defense counsel: It is absolutely essential that the defendant or the defendant's representative be in court from selection of jury to closing arguments. This reduces the impersonality of the corporate giant and the possibility that the plaintiff will call the firm disinterested in what happens.

The trial has a protagonist, an antagonist, a proscenium, and an audience. It is played in three acts: [19]

I. Plaintiff's case. Our stress here is on the expert witness and how he or she should answer questions.
II. Defendant's case. We provide some pointers and cautions.
III. Summation, charge, and verdict. We bring out the importance of the judge.

The presentation of the case is predicated on the legal principles we outlined in Chapter 1. The case rises out of the evidence that is brought into court and the testimony of witnesses. The jury will be asked to apply all the facts to determine a verdict.

FOR THE PLAINTIFF

Let's examine the type of questioning which the plaintiff expert witness may undergo. With a few obvious changes, the defendant's experts will undergo pretty much the same. There are, basically, three parts to the scenario: (1) establishing the expert's qualifications; (2) establishing the details of the accident and subsequent inspections, reports, testing, etc.; and (3) making ready for cross-examination.

The first line of questions bears on the qualifications of the witness. The importance of this phase should not be underestimated: If the judge feels an expert witness has not demonstrated competence in his field, he may halt the expert's testimony at any point and order it stricken from the record. The plaintiff attorney may have hinged his case on testimony that is now inadmissable.

Besides posing the usual questions about profession, employment, engineering experience, societies, and education, the plaintiff attorney should stress experience directly applicable to the type of mechanism involved in the case. Details should be brought out relevant to the expert's experience with similar machines; his knowledge of general principles, general design practices, and the state of the art as it existed when the mechanism was built; and how the expert has kept up with the field. In the area of qualifications, engineers often tend to be modest and overly self-effacing. While some degree of this can be helpful, still the witness should be thorough and complete and leave no room for doubt in the minds of the jury that he has devoted much of his adult life to the general area in which he will be testifying. The plaintiff attorney should stress that the expert's knowledge in the field is not recently acquired for the sake of the lawsuit but rather based on many, many years of general experience in the engineering field.

If the witness never saw the specific type of mechanism before the accident, he will be at a disadvantage when it comes to the state-of-the-art questions. But here refuge may be found in the expert's continuing involvement with similar mechanisms and the field in general—plus the study he has done since becoming involved with the case.

An expert may testify from knowledge gained from study without practical experience in the particular field, but the closer his experience to the field in question, the better for his side. Naked opinion is insufficient, but opinion supported by knowledge is admissable when necessary to give the jury intelligent understanding of the subject matter.

When asked to discuss his inspection of the mechanism, the expert will establish the dates, times, and places the inspections were made. He will then be asked about the findings. At this point the courts will often permit a lengthy narrative, and here the witness can really shine and make his case. Or lose it. He should go over exactly what he did and exactly what he found, providing all proofs necessary—such as X-rays, photos (before and after dissection for examination), graphs, and so forth. He should be prepared to discuss the points in a clear, nontechnical manner so that the jury (and judge) will not be overpowered with a mass of technical verbiage. Doctors frequently spin so many medical terms into their testimony that they do not present as clear a case as they could to the jury; when this happens, the attorney has to pick and choose his questions carefully to bring out the necessary facts. The expert should be prepared to discuss, extensively, the safety devices that were known when the mechanism was built and, if applicable, the safety upgrading that should have taken place during the lifetime of the mechanism up to the time of the accident.

The cross-examination begins when the opposing attorney tries to destroy the impact of the expert's testimony. It is always impossible to predict with accuracy the extent of or thrust of the cross-examination, and sometimes witnesses have had unpleasant surprises. (In the freight elevator case involving time studies, it was the judge who took upon himself the role of cross-examiner.) However, some preparation should be made for attacks along the following lines:

1. An attack on qualifications. Rarely, if ever, has the plaintiff's expert had all his experience and training focused on the subject under discussion in the lawsuit. No engineer can be an expert in all fields, and attempts will always be made to minimize the expert's experience.* If the witness is academically oriented, the cross-examiner bears down on his lack of practical experience. If the reverse is true, he bears down on the lack of academic credentials.

A note to the expert witness: A good thing to bear in mind if you are ever attacked in this way is that no matter what the lawyer asks, you know a thousand times more about the subject than he does—unless the item is new to you and he did more homework than you. Which is a failure on your part.

2. An attack emphasizing that the expert has been retained for the purpose of testifying and is being paid for same. The answer to this is that the expert is being paid for his *time*, and he is answering truthfully as to the findings of his examinations and his opinions.

3. An attack on the expert's lack of direct experience with the particular mechanism under examination. Very few plaintiff experts are available with specific experience in a narrow, de-

---

* The same type of attack may be made on a defense witness.

tailed area. The defendant experts have a much better time of this and have a great advantage with the jury in this area. The answer, again, is for the expert to show how basic principles apply to the mechanism and show familiarity with the basic principles, as well as making an extensive and intensive study of the particular mechanism from the time he is first retained. (The same advice applies to a new manager in an area who finds he will have to testify.)

Here are some general warnings for potential witnesses:

• Listen to each question very carefully—particularly when being cross-examined. Remember the adversary system in our courts: Don't tell anything you have not been asked, pay attention to one question at a time, answer only as much as the question specifically requires (even if a brief answer appears to hurt your side), and leave it to your attorney to protect you.

• If the attorney recites a series of facts and then asks for a "yes" or "no," you should resist the impulse to answer this way except where purely obvious materials are involved (such as your name and employment). Answer each part of the question separately, stating each separate fact in your own words so that you will be able to answer yes to those parts you agree to and no to those you don't. For example:

> QUESTION: Does this widget have a mechanism that goes around and around at over 2,000 RPM?
>
> ANSWER: This widget does have a mechanism and sometimes it does go around at over 2,000 RPM and sometimes it does not.

(The response was broken into two parts to permit the qualifier to be inserted instead of a yes or no that does not "fit.")

• If you can't answer yes or no to a question or break it down into parts, say to the examiner: "I cannot answer the question in that form." Don't be afraid to answer that way over and over again if the attorney persists in propounding complex, unintelligible questions. Some attorneys come prepared with lists of questions they themselves don't understand but which they devised to tire and confuse the witness and commit him to a damaging "yes" or "no." A tired witness starts to volunteer information and allows himself to be trapped into a yes or no answer—then he starts clarifying his answer and reveals more than he should.

• Suppose the examiner says: "Will you agree with me that . . ." and then propounds a hypothetical situation. Proceeding from his assumption, he details his logic and arrives at a conclusion for the situation. The assumption may be (usually is) irrelevant to the case, but the logic is designed to impress the jury—as, naturally, it leads to a conclusion that supports the examiner's case. You should retort with "I cannot agree with you because your assumption is irrelevant (or poor, or whatever)," and stop there. If you start agreeing to or correcting the assumption, you may soon find yourself in a bind; your answers to these questions may repudiate the direct testimony that you gave previously.

• If you sense that a series of questions is leading you down the garden path, you should still continue to give the best possible answers to the questions. Don't try to second-guess the examiner, become a case advocate, or become evasive. Becoming evasive during cross-examination discredits direct testimony in the eyes of the jury. If you answer straightforwardly and a damaging sequence emerges, your own attorney can come back with redirect (additional direct) testimony and work with you to clear up the manner in which "the jury was led astray." Your own attorney will protect you if you do not volunteer information and follow the other guidelines formulated here.

• If you don't remember, say "I don't remember." Opposing attorneys may attempt to "refresh your memory" by priming your mind with carefully chosen facts. If you still don't remember, don't let yourself be bullied into "remembering" something you have just been force-fed. If you do remember the events or facts, then go ahead and answer the question, but take care to repudiate all invalid or irrelevant assumptions and all attempts to "impose testimony."

• Above all, don't play games. If you are a witness in a big case, no matter what kind of country bumpkin you think the other attorney is, assume that his mind is razor sharp and alert to contradictions, weaknesses, or attempts to slant your answers. You are playing in his ballpark, by his rules, for big stakes. He does this work day in and day out; his memory for a sequence of testimony is probably near-fantastic. And you, as you have just gathered, are not going to win this game.

Demonstrations

The plaintiff will usually bring the defective product into the courtroom and will try to arrange some sort of visual pyrotechnics to dazzle the jury and arouse them from any stupor which might have overcome them. Demonstrations are dangerous—a backfire can lose the case. The converse, however, makes them worthwhile.

In presenting a demonstration, the secret is preparedness. Repeat and repeat and repeat the demonstration so that nothing unexpected can go wrong.

Pitfalls

While plaintiff attorneys have many advantages in product liability trials, they are not invulnerable in their claims and presentations to the jury. They tend to choose experts on the basis of price (and then blame them if they don't have enough experience to carry weight in court) and skimp on preparing them. Sometimes they do not even retain one until the trial starts and they see the case going poorly. Or they fail to pay for an adequate and carefully prepared demonstration.

Consider a case in which a riding mower was being driven uphill, the operator shifted to neutral, and the mower rolled backward down the hill. It overturned, and the blades cut off the operator's leg at the knee. The plaintiff's expert maintained that the brake block was worn, as it had two small, $\frac{1}{32}$"-deep grooves in it. This block pressed against the drive sheave, which transmitted power into a gearbox and out to the wheels via a chain. The expert claimed that the wear was so great that no matter how hard the operator pushed on the brake pedal, he could not force the block against the sheave hard enough to prevent backward roll.

The defense engineer prepared four diagrams, all drawn on large artist boards. The first one showed the engine turning the belt which turned the sheave; it showed the sheave transmitting power into the gear box, the arrangement of the gears, the shifting apparatus, and the braking assembly. The diagram is not shown here because the defense attorney destroyed it the minute he saw it. The engineer then drew Figure 4. The defense attorney vetoed the use of this diagram as well. The engineer then drew Figures 5 and 6. Only Figure 6 was used.

Why? Figure 6 and the actual brake block were used to win the case and the others suppressed because the other diagrams show too clearly that the braking is transmitted through the sheave, the gear case, and the chain mechanism. When the operator shifted to neutral, there was no gear connection between the sheave and the wheels—hence, no brakes. The real problem was this design defect.

In court, the puny grooves in the brake block were used to make a laughingstock of the plaintiff engineer—grooves are to be expected with a normal wear pattern. What the plaintiff engineer did not discover, and the defense did not tell him, is that there were no brakes on that mower when the operator shifted to neutral going up the hill.

In a similar case, a machine spit a rock out of its mechanism. Plaintiff claimed that he was hurt—even though he was 150 feet away from the machine. The judge refused to believe (and the plaintiff expert did not convince) that this could happen and told the plaintiff to accept a settlement or he would find against him—throw the case out of court for lack of ability to show it could happen. The settlement was for medical and other bills. In actuality, the defendant had discovered with some sophisticated tests and calculations that this machine would fling a rock 750–850 feet; but the defendant was under no requirement to reveal what he had found and the settlement went through. Remember the adversary system!

FIGURE 4. Riding mower sheave and brake mechanism.

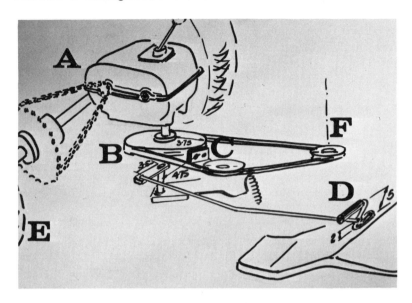

A: Gear box   C: Brake block   E: Mower tire
B: Drive sheave   D: Brake pedal   F: Engine pulley

FIGURE 5. Outline of riding mower brake mechanism.

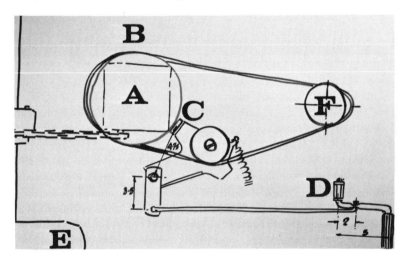

FIGURE 6. Bare outline of riding mower brake mechanism.

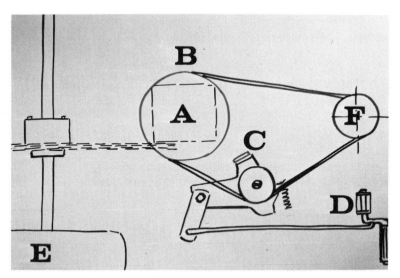

FOR THE DEFENSE

In many suits, the plaintiff will try to "join all the parties"—that is, call into court everyone who had anything to do with putting the product into the stream of commerce and servicing it thereafter. In court, the multiple defendants will become so wrapped up in shifting the blame to each other that plaintiff's counsel can often sit back and let the other side kill its own defense.

It is therefore prudent for all parties handling a product to arrange beforehand to avoid cross-suits, to arrange liability in advance, and to plan a course of action in the event of a product liability claim.[20] One way to do this is through purchase orders or legal contracts in which one party accepts liability and the other agrees to get behind him for a unified defense.

The defense attorney marshals the full resources of the defendant firm and, when an entire industry feels it is vulnerable in a case, even experts supplied by competing firms. He cross-examines each plaintiff witness and tries, without antagonizing the jury, to impeach the witnesses' credibility.

His own witnesses and demonstrations should be carefully chosen. Frequently company personnel will have had no court experience. They should be given a day or two off to visit a local courtroom and learn what to expect.

The company expert who has had no court experience can still be invaluable if he is articulate, flexible, and can put engineering into lay terms. Sometimes he does not even have to be articulate. One such company man had a bad stutter. It took two and a half hours to obtain thirty minutes of testimony from him. Cross-examination proved utterly frustrating to the plaintiff attorney. The case was won because the jury got the impression that he must be the foremost expert in the field or they would not have been subjected to such an experience.

There are company experts who do nothing but travel around and testify in case after case against plaintiffs who sue alleging defects in such products as tires, soft drinks, and so forth. These experts' specialized knowledge and experience with the product can be devastating when matched against the qualifications of the plaintiff's experts, and the company person often has the ability to call on all the super-specialists he needs to help him.

In addition to the do's and don'ts noted under "For the Plaintiff," the following are instructive for defendants:

• Although component cost is of prime importance to the manufacturer, and dictates the eventual floor to the selling price (and profits), the defense witness should avoid discussing component costs as much as possible. Here is an example of what can happen when component costs are brought up: A machine did not switch off when the handle was released and an operator was hurt. Question by plaintiff attorney (on cross-examination): "Why wasn't a dead man's [automatic cutoff] switch used?" Answer by defendant manager: "The dead man's switch cost 40 cents per unit more." Plaintiff attorney was able to get a lot of mileage with the jury by comparing his client's injuries with a 40-cent switch.

The witness is advised to answer direct questions right to

the point, but volunteer nothing. He should prepare for questions along this line by discussing the individual case in a very thorough manner with his attorney.

• The witness should avoid having answers forced out of him regarding the expected life of a product or component, especially in a safety switch application. If the item does not have a specific life expectancy, the witness should remain adamant in his answers and say repeatedly that failure of the item does not occur at a specific time.

In one court situation, the plaintiff attorney was cross-examining a defendant engineer about the life expectancy of a safety switch. He wanted the engineer to put an expected life on the switch, so he started with small numbers (ones, tens, hundreds) and kept going higher and higher. "Will the switch fail at a thousand operations?" "No!" "Will the switch fail at one hundred thousand operations?" "No!" "Will it fail at a million?" Whereupon the tired engineer, anxious to bring the questions to an end, said, "Yes!"

The attorney then demonstrated on a blackboard that this switch operated 60 times per hour, 8 to 12 hours per day. The number became a reality, and liability was established.

• Photos, charts, and diagrams must be carefully planned so as not to give the opposition grist for its mill. The riding mower example given earlier is an extreme example of how this may work.

• A demonstration is enjoyed by the jury and takes them away from scientific testimony which goes on ad nauseam. Managers and engineers should give some thought to whether a cutaway or a brand new product similar to the one that caused the problem should be used. The case and the product dictate the method.

If the defense attorney does decide to use a manufactured product similar to the one that injured the claimant, he should make absolutely sure that:

1. The product is perfect.
2. It operates flawlessly.
3. It has been tested and retested (but not "to death").

4. The courtroom demonstrator has used and used and used it and is completely familiar with every detail.

Considering what we have written about demonstrations, is it possible that any company attorney would let an unprepared demonstration get into the courtroom? Let the record speak for itself: In one case defense counsel brought in a Bureau of Mines expert to testify that a particular gas mask was safe—it could not have caused a death. The expert was never shown the actual mask until, in court, he was asked to put it on and demonstrate its safety. The expert recoiled. "Not me; I'd never put on such a mask. It's a killer!"

• The defendant should remain alert for trial testimony which appears false, misleading, or technically inaccurate. While his attorney will usually pick this up and use appropriate legal objections, the defendant may hear something that the attorney missed. The two should have discussed a plan of action for such a situation beforehand, but if they did not, the defendant may want to quietly and discreetly warn his attorney. Sometimes the attorney will allow such testimony to go by for the moment and later use it to totally impeach everything the witness has said to support his side.

• Defense counsel should be aware that the adversary party may try to present to the jury a great deal of material even if it knows some or most of it will be ruled inadmissable evidence. We discussed earlier the problem of objectionable material in a deposition; its ramifications are broader here. There is much research on criminal trials leading us to believe that when the judge tells the jury to "forget and not consider what you just heard," the jury does not do so.[21] The same is probably true for civil trials: The testimony which is stricken from the record is not erased from the jurors' minds and, especially in a "weak" case, will help tip the scales in one way or the other.[22] Sue and Smith write: "It appears that the biasing effect of inadmissable evidence is greatest when there is little other evidence on which to make a decision. The controversial evidence then becomes quite salient in a juror's mind."[23]

One court in Ohio tried videotaping a trial, weeding out the inadmissable or irrelevant testimony, and then showing the tape to a jury for the verdict. The weeding was done by opposing counsel and the judge. This approach is being given experimental attention and may someday be used for depositions as well.

• Direct examination of the defense witnesses comes after the plaintiff has put on display all his proof that something was defective and caused the accident. Therefore, even if not all the witnesses were allowed to remain in the courtroom while other testimony was being given, the defense attorney can still brief them on what has been alleged and what to expect. There should be no surprises; preparation of witnesses should be thorough.

THE SUMMATION, CHARGE, AND VERDICT

After both sides have exhausted the legal pyrotechnics available, they sum up their cases to the jury. The judge charges (instructs) the jury on the laws which apply to the case and their responsibility in finding on the evidence.

At this point, it is instructive to point out that the plaintiff bore the burden of proving there was a case—even as he conducted his scenario. The judge is not a passive spectator. If he feels that the plaintiff attorney presented a case in which the jury was not even given food for thought regarding the negligence of the defendant, he can dismiss the case right there—or anywhere else along the line. He will not allow the plaintiff to cross-examine the defendant's witnesses and establish a case by tripping them up if the plaintiff has not been able to build his own case. He may dismiss the case after each side has made its presentations and summaries; he may set aside a jury verdict as not founded on the facts; he may knock down the size of the jury's damage award. Belli calls the judge "the thirteenth juror" —a person who has tremendous power in reversing a verdict or reducing its benefits to the plaintiff.[24]

Sometimes the court may double or treble the award the plaintiff justifiably should get. These are punitive damages—a form of fine against the defendant. The plaintiff attorney will ask the jury for such damages if he has been able to prove that:

1. The manufacturer was aware of a defect in the product.
2. The manufacturer attempted to conceal the defect or deliberately misrepresented the product to the public.

Finally, if one side is unhappy with the verdict it can appeal the case to a higher court, claiming that some judicial error occurred. The appeals court will examine the transcripts, the lawyers' brief, and the evidence. It can order a new trial, reduce the award (it rarely increases it), or throw the case out of court.

More and more, appeals courts have become the arm of consumer advocates and have been imposing further and further legal duties upon manufacturers. Certain legal doctrines that are burdensome to manufacturers were first framed by appeals courts—which, in effect, have been taking over the roles of various state and federal legislatures. However, some state appeals courts confine their attention exclusively to the size of the award and take no exceptions to the factual findings of juries.

In sum, therefore, the trial court is still the main battleground and the arena in which all best efforts are expended. In fact, some judges—when trying a case without a jury—take so much care in writing their decisions intensively and comprehensively that they effectively shut off all avenues of appeal. They do not want to be overturned, so they allow no room for errors.

CONCLUSION

We have reviewed the trial primarily from the standpoint of witnesses—expert witnesses and participating managers—and have tried to show what they will encounter. We do not claim to have covered all that witnesses should know, and there is no substitute for preparation. But in working with an attorney, the prospective witness will now have a good idea of the "rules of the game" and how he or she should behave in situations not previously foreseen.

REFERENCES

1. M. M. Cheatham, "The Lawyer's Role and Surroundings," *Rocky Mountain Law Review,* Vol. 25, No. 405 (1953), p. 409.
2. Chester L. Karrass, *The Negotiating Game* (New York: World Publishing Company, 1970), p. 4.
3. Ibid., pp. 17–25.
4. Ibid., p. 21.
5. Melvin M. Belli, *Ready for the Plaintiff* (New York: Henry Holt and Company, 1956), p. 213.
6. Louis Nizer, *My Life in Court* (Garden City, N.Y.: Doubleday & Company, 1961), p. 415.
7. *The Wall Street Journal,* November 27, 1973, p. 12.
8. Nizer, op. cit.
9. Ibid., p. 416.
10. James W. Jeans, "Settlement of Personal Injury Claims," *Journal of the Bar Association of Kansas,* Vol. 37, No. 79 (Summer 1968).
11. Hans Zeisel, Harry Kalven, Jr., and Bernard Buchholz, *Delay in the Court* (Boston: Little, Brown & Company, 1959), Chapter 12.
12. Richard J. Leonard, "The Preparation and Use of Witnesses," *The Practical Lawyer,* Vol. 16, No. 1 (January 1970), p. 43.
13. Ibid., p. 46.
14. John E. Simonett, "The Trial as One of the Performing Arts," *American Bar Association Journal,* Vol. 52 (December 1966), p. 1145. Also: Jonathan R. Laing, "For the Defense: Keeping Verdicts Low in Personal Injury Suits Takes Specialized Skills," *The Wall Street Journal,* July 5, 1973, p. 1.
15. Laing, op. cit.
16. Ibid., p. 17.
17. Robert Begam, "Jury Selection." *ATL Counseling Cassettes,* Vol. 4, No. 3, Association of Trial Lawyers of America, 1974.
18. Cited in ibid.
19. Simonett, op. cit.
20. Clare E. Wise, "Carnage in the Courtroom," *Machine Design* (May 4, 1972), p. 24.

21. Stanley Sue and Ronald E. Smith, "How Not to Get a Fair Trial: Inadmissable Evidence and Pretrial Publicity," *Psychology Today* (May 1974), pp. 86–90.
22. Ibid., p. 90.
23. Ibid.
24. Belli, op. cit., p. 234.

5

INSURANCE

The Big Buffer?

In this chapter we will focus on educating the executive with regard to the possible consequences of inadequate insurance coverage and the extent to which insurance is actually a buffer between the plaintiff and the insured company's resources. We will cover some of the basic principles of insurance, difficulties in purchasing it, and loopholes that might leave one without coverage. We will also advise on methods of improving the scope and reducing the cost of product liability insurance.

We recognize that such insurance is usually purchased as part of a general, comprehensive liability policy. But we will confine our discussion here to the product liability part, leaving the rest for other texts.

SOME BASICS ABOUT INSURANCE

Early Chinese merchants preparing to ship goods down the treacherous Yangtze River adopted a clever stratagem. They distributed their cargoes among all the boats going at one time. Thus, if any one boat was lost, the merchants involved lost only a small portion of their entire shipments. Simple cooperation saved many of the merchants from ruin and increased the profits for all.[1]

If we now define risk as the probability of loss of an individual object, we see that the risk virtually disappears with a large number of participating merchants. In the same way, the commercial insurance firm accepts a large number of individuals (known as insureds or assureds) and pools their combined risks in order to minimize the impact on any one. The insurer takes moneys from each merchant to cover the expected losses, but with the combination method the individual insurer is taking little risk, except where:

1. All the boats go down in a single storm.
2. Some of the objects are indivisible and thus represent such large values on a single boat that a loss would, indeed, affect the insurer.
3. A large number of the boats are inexpertly manned, improperly maintained, or otherwise unseaworthy and go under at the slightest unexpected event.

Some large companies with extensive product lines have what is known as a spread-of-risk within their own organization and may non-insure or self-insure because no single product line is large enough to significantly affect the assets or earning power of the corporation as a whole. A company policy of non-insurance exists when the company elects to absorb product liability losses out of its yearly earnings cash flow. Some companies put aside a "rainy day fund" whose level is more influenced by executive intuition than by any reasoned examination of likely losses; Greene labels such funds as just another form of non-insurance.[2] In self-insurance, however, there is a carefully established and managed financial reserve backing the product. Where hundreds of thousands of a given product are out on the market over a period of time, one can predict with reasonable certainty the magnitude of damage or loss from such a "pool."

When management decides to self-insure, it predicts the probability of suffering a lawsuit, the possible verdict range, and the number of suits per year. It then sets aside a highly liquid reserve (investment reserve) to cover this exposure. Management, in effect, sets up an internal insurance plan which must perform all the necessary functions of an insurance firm—such as premium collections to replenish the fund and investment management—lest it slip unwittingly into the non-insured category.

To protect themselves against unforeseen catastrophes, self-insured companies transfer some of the risks to commercial insurers through what is known as "surplus" or "excess" insurance coverage. In this situation the insurer sets up his own fund to cover the risks of the insured and then collects a yearly fee for this coverage. When the loss rate cannot be predicted accurately or the number of products in the pool is small, then as much of the risk as possible is transferred to the insurance company.

A company may be non-insured because at some point in time someone in the company elected to bear any foreseeable loss out of the working capital of the company. Such an attitude may well have developed in a state jurisdiction where juries were extremely conservative and the interpretation of the law favored the company. In some cases, the impact of taxes further cushions the possible financial blows to the company. It is not unusual, therefore, for a company to continue such a policy even when it should be reconsidered in the light of growing product liability litigation.

To minimize the risk, both the insured and the insurer will engage in loss-prevention activities (make the Yangtze boats more seaworthy). These may consist of (1) eliminating a product line, e.g., certain types of flammable nightwear; (2) redesigning a product to make an accident virtually impossible—for example, the use of static mixing tubes for liquids instead of conventional motor-driven apparatuses; and (3) a host of other actions to be covered in the next chapter.

DIFFICULTIES IN PURCHASING INSURANCE

One of the fundamental worries the individual company, or its top management, has is the uncertainty as to whether or not a loss will actually be covered by the insurance program. Although management may do everything in its power to reduce the probability of incurring a product liability suit, there is no way of knowing from which of a multitude of products, sold over many years on a worldwide basis, litigation may be generated. If the possibility of a serious financial loss exists, even though its probability is small, the company should take steps to avoid the impact through purchase of product liability insurance or other methods of risk avoidance or transfer.

Yet, insurance is one of the most difficult commodities a company has to purchase on the open market. Some of the reasons are as follows:

1. The insurance company expects to make a profit on its dealings with its clients. The insurer tries to establish the principle of large numbers and evaluate realistically the risks for which it attempts to insure. To do this, it inserts clauses in its insurance which are designed to protect it in the event of miscalculation or misunderstanding. Its contract with the insured is drawn up in legal terminology which will stand up in a court trial. The insurer also tries to protect itself against certain losses which are *not* accidental or unforeseen or unintentional. For example, it resents having the company actually make a profit from the insurance industry through the loss-collection process. Thus, there are many clauses in the traditional insurance policy wherein the insurer defines its side of the contract to eliminate these items.

The insurer wants to be able to estimate the extent of a loss in order to underwrite the risk before the event, and also to provide for a careful accounting after a loss occurs. Thus the insurer needs to know as much as possible about the inherent dangers or characteristics of a product, including the effects of mere misuse of it. It needs to know, for example, whether a simple fertilizer, harmless under normal conditions, can explode under certain unfavorable storage conditions.

The insurer also wants to avoid catastrophic losses. Earlier, it was mentioned that design cases were the ones hardest fought in the courts: Proving a design is bad hurts the whole class of products incorporating that design, and a string of suits can develop. (This is equivalent to all the boats sinking beneath the Yangtze.) Some insurance companies do not cover design error, but whether it is covered or not, certain clauses will be inserted to clarify the intent and basically protect the insurer. The language of such clauses becomes more complex every day, and when tested in the courts is found wanting and frequently unsatisfactory to both insured and insurer.

2. There is big money at stake. More and larger-value cases confront the insurance industry as plaintiff attorneys become better at trying them. Product liability is a relatively new field, and the legal profession is only at the bottom of the learning curve. Client-attorney expectations, the march of the consumer, and other factors are causing an ever increasing number of people and companies to turn to the courts to rectify perceived wrongs. Companies have become popular legal targets, and transferring this risk to the insurance industry is becoming increasingly costly.

3. A serious problem in the purchase of insurance is the apparent divided loyalty of the broker. Presumably he works for both the insured and the insurer, but traditionally his compensation is determined and actually paid by the insurer. While he does not want to lose your business, you may represent only one of a large number of his customers, particularly if the insurance underwriter or insurance firm is one of a relatively small number of firms which will write product liability insurance at all.

Many brokers are not really professionals in the product liability field. They generally handle a broad range of policies, which forces them to concentrate on the sales aspects of all rather than those matters of prime concern to the insured—namely, coverage, exclusions, limitations, improvements, and broadening of coverage with respect to product liability insurance. Unfortunately, a situation develops in which critical information is transferred between two contracting parties, the underwriter and the insured, through a nonspecialist. The manager who calls a broker for a detailed response to questions about limitations in his coverage will frequently find that he gets conflicting interpretations over a period of time, or none at all.

Thus, the closer you can get to a meeting of minds with the

underwriter by direct personal contact, the better. If you represent a very large company you may already have self-insured many of these risks, or you may be participating in an industry-wide plan or be dealing directly with underwriters—making such a meeting of the minds much easier than it is for a small company.

4. Managers make most decisions by what March and Simon call "satisficing." [3] They make a continuous search for increasingly better alternatives, bearing in mind the improvement to be attained versus the time expended and the press of other matters. They stop searching when they find an alternative yielding a result which is "satisfactory" and "sufficient." [4] The difficulty with insurance, however, is that a full range of options is not displayed. The search is deliberately arduous; the insurance firm sells what is good for it and its reinsurers, as opposed to what is good for the insured customer. The insurance buyer may be well aware that he has not been exposed to all permutations of contracts and that he is probably satisficing at higher premiums and lesser coverage, but he cannot afford the time or energy to unearth something better.

5. Finally, many companies fail to recognize that purchasing insurance has become a profession. The largest companies have begun to employ risk managers, but most, unfortunately, allow this assignment to fall to a financial vice president or an operating manager who merely reviews the insurance policies as they come up for annual renewal. Other firms leave it to the broker, who may be handling everything from workmen's compensation to the insurance on the company limousine. In the latter case, the manager purchasing the insurance for his company has relegated his decision on what he needs to the judgment of an outsider who may have a conflict of interest or lack specialized knowledge.

LIMITATIONS OF INSURANCE COVERAGE

Insufficient or inappropriate coverage that a company has purchased for itself, or assumed by defaults in decision making, is a time bomb which explodes after a claim is launched against it. Prior to this event, as we have indicated, review of coverage is all too frequently done by sales agents or busy people with multiple duties. After the event, the insured finally gets a review of coverage by highly experienced people—the insurance adjusters. Their first task is to see if the insured really does have coverage for "this type of claim," and their second is to minimize the financial impact on the insurer who engages them. Quite frequently the company will discover that its own exposure is far greater than was thought, with management having neglected to review its policy adequately.

But even if the insurance buyer makes the most conscientious attempts to purchase and maintain proper coverage, he or she occasionally gets unpleasant surprises from the insurer. Some of them may be traced to the following:

1. Insurance firms are likely to prejudge claims and disclaim coverage even before all the facts are uncovered. The insurance adjuster or attorneys will examine the complaint or ask for a bill of particulars from the plaintiff. If the plaintiff alleges a design defect, the insurer will frequently deny defense or indemnity, stating that the policy does not cover design defects and the company will have to bear its own costs in the defense and resulting damages.

Management's proper response is to demand that the case not be prejudged as to coverage. If you are so involved, arrange to have your in-house legal staff or retained counsel ride herd over the insurance firm, to (1) see to it that the insurer does not instruct its legal counsel "to get us off the hook"; (2) assure complete follow-through and legal defense, because it may turn out in court that a design case (which might have merited no coverage) involved a construction defect or inadequate testing, either of which does merit coverage; and (3) document all costs of this defense. If, later, the facts justify the insurance firm stepping aside, your company can reimburse it for costs and retain the same counsel, thus insuring continuity in defense. This course of action is the one generally prescribed for dealing with all reputable insurers where coverage is disputed.

2. You failed to comply with certain policy requirements.

You may have failed to notify the insurer of a claim within a certain number of days after receipt, or failed to provide documentation of your manufacturing processes as agreed. Or you may have hindered an insurance audit by noncooperation, which could be interpreted as concealment. An insurance firm providing broad coverage under a general liability policy generally conducts an audit once a year, in which it reexamines your product lines and any additional claims incurred over the year. Such reviews frequently result in premium increases and occasionally in cutbacks in coverage or specific deletions of certain products from the coverage.

A serious problem arises in failure to report a claim. Sometimes you may not know that a claim has been entered against a dealer or distributor which will, eventually, involve you. If you did not know of the claim, you could not have notified the insurer within the usual 30-day period. The insurer provides for this by allowing you to obtain an administrative waiver of the time limit for reporting. But what if the policy in force at the time of the accident has expired, and you now have a new one? Did you or did you not have coverage when that particular accident took place? Be careful not to dispose of your old policies. Keep them to prove that you have had coverage over a long period of time with no gaps. In the past, it was customary to keep policies seven or eight years, but now it is prudent to hold them much longer, even indefinitely, by proper storage or on microfilm.

3. You may have elected to absorb a high-level deductible on your policy, feeling that the aggregate claims would make an acceptable impact on the yearly financial statement. The insurer may have imposed this deductible level because you had been suffering numerous claims. However, the sum of the actual payouts plus associated legal costs may total a far higher amount than you expected. If a big payout year happens to coincide with a revenue downturn, the impact on the firm's profit and loss statement may necessitate an embarrassing footnote to the annual report. The dip in profit and the increasing deductibles will strike potential lenders as symptoms of deeper troubles, and may result in a damaged credit rating or a lower price/earnings ratio on the stock market.

4. Unwise or inadequate policy limits provide a source of grief to many insureds. In the old days, a person's life might have been worth up to a quarter of a million dollars. Today, awards exceeding a million dollars—especially in injury cases and in commercial mishaps—are not uncommon. Much higher limits are desirable today. Often, however, a change in times and climate does not evoke a change in coverage. Some companies fall into a yearly renewal pattern, or their desire not to increase the premium costs is coupled with executive shortcomings.

5. You failed to take account of "sistership liability." Suppose your firm makes fuel pumps for aircraft. One or two pumps fail, and tests show a key component is at fault. You might be liable for payment to have every pump in every airplane pulled and the component replaced because a reasonable expectation exists that a failure in one is a prelude to failure in all. Furthermore, you will be exposed to a damage suit by the airlines and other aircraft owners for every hour of downtime they may suffer. Unless you have specific coverage for this particular liability, it will appear as a "sistership exclusion" somewhere in your standard policy. That means the insurance firm won't pay for the pulling, the component replacement, or the damage suits therefrom. Just where the peculiar name "sistership exclusion" comes from is unclear, but its impact can be deadly indeed.

6. Closely allied to sistership insurance is recall and withdrawal insurance, which has gradually been removed from insurance policies unless it is specifically endorsed and a separate premium is paid. Under the Consumer Product Safety Act, a manufacturer must notify the Consumer Product Safety Commission within 24 hours of discovering that something he produced and sold represents "a substantial product hazard." [5] Recall insurance pays for advertising (asking people to send in the product, or telling them to throw it away) and also pays for the costs of getting out into the field and recovering the product. Recall policies usually do not include the actual costs of shipping the products back to the factory or safely destroying them. Where the defective product is a chemical, for example, the shipping and destruction can be quite costly. For this, special coverage known as withdrawal insurance is needed.

7. You failed to get "business risk" insurance. Was the bodily injury or property damage caused by a mistake of top management? If it was, and if your policy excludes business-risk insurance (i.e., you did not pay an extra premium to have it included), there is no coverage. Management may overrate a product's capacity to perform or make a mistake in a formulation, thinking, for example, that one combination of chemicals would substitute adequately for another. Exclusion of business risk from the standard policy is another effort of insurers to prevent insured managers from transferring certain unintended risks to the insurance industry and profiting thereby. As noted before, unavoidable or unexpected failures are proper subjects for normal coverage.

8. Your company carelessly assumed more liability than management thought it was vulnerable to. In signing a particular contract with a hot sales prospect, you may have agreed in the contract to be legally responsible for extra services, or to "hold harmless" the purchaser for claims against him, or to set up and test a complex machine outside the range of your normal capabilities. Unless you have specific coverage for such "contractual liability," you may find yourself without coverage—or, at the very least, in a bad hassle with the insurer should something go wrong.

Closely allied to assuming liability by contract is the "vendor's endorsement." Here, a parent company or a large customer or supplier helps a smaller company reduce its insurance premiums. The larger company pays for coverage of the vendor for all foreseeable mishaps to the product and its users. This endorsement is frequently used when the vendor is an important part of the firm's supply or distribution chain and the vendor's negligence or defense will most likely involve the bigger company as well. The problem here is that the vendor's plant, warehouse, and stores are out of the direct control of the larger company. The vendor may not be refrigerating pharmaceutical products as he promised to do; he may be taking design and production shortcuts you are not aware of; he may leave off protective safeguards from certain machinery or allow the purchaser to exercise a dangerous option; he may be showing you one set of systems and procedures while "doing his own thing" when you are not around. The first time these or other differences come out in court, you may lose your entire coverage on the product for future cases, or face a complete denial of coverage starting with the claim you have already received.

9. You may have overlooked territorial limitations of coverage. Unless you specifically provide such coverage, you may find yourself inadequately protected in the following situations:

(a) A foreign purchaser engages counsel and sues in the United States for a product produced in the United States.

(b) A foreign purchaser sues one of your offices in his own or the nearest foreign country for a product produced in the United States.

(c) Your product was produced outside the United States by one of your foreign divisions, and you are sued in that or another country.

(d) Your product was produced outside the United States by one of your foreign divisions, and claims are brought against the home office in the United States.

The standard policy covers the insured's legal liability against bodily injury or property damage arising from products manufactured, sold, distributed, or leased in the United States of America, its territories or possessions, Canada, or international waters or airspace—provided the bodily injury or property damage does not occur in the course of travel or transportation to or from any other country or state and provided the original suit is brought within such territory.

Product litigation is now developing overseas as it did here more than a decade ago. In some countries a consumer can seek a state or national indictment of a company for violating a criminal statute regarding the merchantability of its product. If the company is found guilty, the consumer can use this verdict in a civil action. Product liability law in Europe varies by country, but gradually the old legal interpretations and theories are breaking down to favor the consumers' interests.

In Belgium, for example, contractual liability is presently

limited by time, and tort claims require plaintiff proof. In Germany the liability both in contract and in tort depends upon who was responsible for a defect, but in certain cases the burden of proof has strangely shifted from plaintiff to defendant. In Italy there is a very limited basis for product liability by contract; the plaintiff must prove negligence. But this too is changing to shift more of the burden onto the defendant, who must prove he did nothing wrong. In Sweden, product liability law is still being formulated. In the Netherlands, rethinking and changes are under way in the law because of the famous thalidomide cases, but as yet the plaintiff must prove liability arising through responsibility for a defect. In the United States there is no liability without proof of responsibility for a defect.

What is common practice in the United States may be unethical or illegal in other countries. For example, the American concept of contingency fees * (not paying if you lose the case, but paying a percentage of the award if you win) is considered unethical throughout Europe, the United Kingdom, and Canada. In most of those countries, the loser pays the legal fees of the opposing side as well as his own. In the United States, the loser cannot be sued by the opposition for recovery of its attorney's fees.

Consider again the four situations listed on page 131. Types (b) and (d) deserve particular mention because they are the most common. As an example of a type (b) case, the liability for an accident in France arising out of a defective machine manufactured in the United States would not be covered under the standard policy if a subsidiary or branch office of the company was sued in Paris. Likewise, a machine or component part manufactured in Sweden and shipped to the United States would be excluded from coverage under the standard policies, since it was manufactured outside the territories described in the policy (a type (d) case). An endorsement, therefore, should be added to most policies to specifically cover an original suit brought anywhere, and to specifically include products produced anywhere in

* Legal in all states except New Hampshire.

the world, provided that the suit is brought within the United States, its territories or possessions, Canada, or international waters or airspace.

Many companies pay insurance premiums on the basis of worldwide coverage, but the policy must be properly worded. If the product has any possibility at all of going to a foreign country, or incorporates foreign parts (or is liable to do so), coverage is the prudent manager's method of dealing with the situations outlined above. Don't depend on coverage purchased by foreign subsidiaries unless and until you have checked it out to see that there are no gaps between the coverage the home office has and that purchased by the subsidiary. Check and recheck for coverage of the four situations outlined earlier.

10. Punitive damages are recognized in many states but are not normally included in the standard policy. The states that recognize punitive damages consider them to be in the nature of compensation for insult and indignity to the feelings of persons arising from aggravated circumstances, and thus compensation for personal injury rather than bodily injury. Endorsements can be specifically tailored to cover all situations except those in which the insured has displayed malicious, willful, wanton, and reckless disregard for others. Punitive damages are usually three times the regular damages.

While product liability punitive damages are not yet a regularly encountered threat to the average company, consumerism and the increasing questioning of company motives will have their effects in the courtroom. Lack of this coverage could, overnight, become very costly.

11. A new or unnoticed exclusion may have been inserted in your policy when it was renewed. Each renewal should be treated with all the care due a new contract, and therefore each new policy should be carefully examined to determine the meanings of every change that has taken place. New riders, endorsements, exclusions, and other revisions are not simply to be filed away but rather should be given complete review in the context of the old material. Anything which is unclear must be explained by the insurer to your satisfaction.

CLAIMS AND THE ROLE OF THE INSURER

Assuming you did not fall prey to any of the 11 problems outlined above, the insurance firm will now be defending you, the client, in the event of a product liability suit. Broadly stated, the insurance firm's role is to retain counsel (subject to your veto if you retained that right in your policy) and to pay all costs to mitigate, defend, and settle all claims up to the limits stated in the policy.

Let us caution at this point that you and your attorney should establish a procedure to be followed throughout your organization and his whenever a threat to sue, a claim in a letter, or a legal summons is received. There may even be a possible source of litigation in a simple question about a product or its use. There are many ifs, ands, and buts concerning who in the company should be notified, precisely when and how the insurer should be notified, and who actually should convey the material to the in-house or retained counsel. We could write a separate law book on this subject and still miss considering certain essential aspects of your operation. To indicate the type of complexities we have in mind: Under some circumstances (such as a large or serious claim) the directors of the company must learn about the matter; under other circumstances your attorney may want them to be able, if necessary, to legitimately claim ignorance. Under some circumstances the company may elect to fight every case, even though fully covered, and call on the insurer only in catastrophic situations. In other cases, the tiniest claim is bucked to the insurer immediately. The need for precision in drafting the procedures for who tells what and when upon receipt of a threat or claim is so important that we again recommend you meet with your attorney to establish appropriate ground rules. Get these rules into the procedures manuals, and have personnel indoctrinated.

In-house or retained counsel (unless your insurance department specifically has the job and legal expertise) is your agent to see that the defense is properly handled by the insurer. He should (1) check on who the insurance firm has chosen to defend the case and express his opinions about the choice to top management; or (2) get the insurance firm to assign the defense to him—not an unusual practice in very large firms or in highly technical cases requiring extreme legal specialization and experience with the particular client.

The defense attorney and the in-house counsel should work together to the extent that the case requires. From the viewpoint of the defendant company, a close relationship is most desirable for a number of reasons, some of which follow.

The company will be assembling all the files requested by the defense, including the genealogy of the product, all complaints, and all other items mentioned in previous chapters. In-house counsel, familiar with the firm and the legalities of the case, can help make this as smooth and economical a process as possible.

The defense attorney and the technical people in the firm may have little or no rapport—and occasionally no desire at all to communicate. If the designers, production people, and other personnel view the outsider from the insurance firm as management's tool not only to fight the case but to allocate blame, the problems are obviously compounded. Again, the in-house attorney—who should be no stranger—will bridge the gap.

In-house counsel must be alert to prevent defense brinkmanship. Here the defense attorney conducts his case only by responding to requests from the plaintiff. Defense feels he can use a facade and settle before trial, so why bother with all the behind-the-scenes details. Or brinkmanship may be practiced in this form: The defense gathers a huge file with hundreds of papers, drawings, statements, models, and demonstrations. Defense counsel shows up at the plant one day before the trial, grabs the file, and promises to "study it." He expects to settle the case—and he has a lot of other work to do—so he is going to use the file and the accoutrements for facing down the other side rather than for more preparation. Of course, defense engineers and other personnel then get a hurry-up call to the witness stand when the strategy backfires.

Despite thousands of man-hours spent in preparation behind the scenes, more good cases are lost by the defense through unprepared witnesses and attorneys than many an insurer will care to admit. The company's in-house counsel or retained counsel must be sure that the insurer's defense attorney is being kept up to date as all materials are gathered, that all organization personnel know the part they are to play in the case, and that adequate effort is being exercised by defense attorneys to do the best possible job. In-house counsel should report to top management any deviations he feels are taking place from the highest possible levels of defense performance.

The reader may wonder why the insurance firm cannot be depended on to do the best job all the time. Frequently the insurer and the insured have divergent concerns. The insurer cannot focus on your claim alone: He runs a business with thousands of claims to be monitored, and he may take the attitude that overall defense-cost limitation is paramount.* What might to you be a major blot on your company reputation is part of an assembly-line operation to many insurers. How well a particular insurer monitors its operations and minimizes the deficiencies of its assembly-line approach determines how well you will be served, and is determined, in turn, by how seriously the insurer takes its obligations. The more reputable insurers take their responsibilities quite seriously, and have earned their high esteem.

THE INSURER'S ACTIONS AFTER CASE DISPOSAL

After the legal proceedings have been completed in a case, the insurance underwriter may pay you a visit. If he has a loss-prevention unit or facility, he most certainly will be flanked by a team that will want to become more familiar with your business —perhaps to a dismaying degree. Your alternative to admitting them is, of course, policy cancellation.

The insurer may withdraw coverage as soon as your policy expires. This means you had what is loosely termed "first bite

---

* In the long run, defense-cost limitation may also serve the interests of the insured. If there are many claims against a product and defense costs are high, up go the premiums, deductibles, exclusions, and limitations. Even entire policies may be canceled.

coverage," in which the insurance firm says, "We covered you and saved you from the first bite, but the second one is on you. Now that you've been put on notice that your product is dangerous, the dangerous aspects, or the product itself, must be eliminated before we will restore the coverage." If, by the way, the insurance firm in defending a case against you digs up a series of complaints and indications that you had ample notice your product was dangerous but did nothing about it, the insurer may not even absorb the first bite.

The insuring process, as is the case with other industries, is basically a cost/benefit program for the insurer. If you have more exposure than someone else, you have to pay more to transfer that risk—and obviously a record of losses on a product is proof positive of a greater exposure. Your payment to the carrier is predicated on the basic philosophy that the insurance firm ultimately sells back to you your own claims, except for the multimillion-dollar catastrophe. This is particularly true for the sophisticated buyer who purchases insurance on a cost-plus basis. The claims filed against your insurer, and paid in your behalf, will wind up in premium payments upon renewal of the policy. When administrative expenses, profits, and fees are taken into account, you may be paying two dollars or more for every dollar of loss or claim against you.

The insurance firm may force you to recall products or withdraw them completely from the market, upon threat of policy cancellation. They may even reexamine all the other policies you hold with them to see if you truly merit their comprehensive general liability coverage. Your financial people will be most concerned when certificates of insurance, covering assets and earnings pledged as part of debt collateral, come under examination.

A POSITIVE APPROACH TO PRODUCT LIABILITY INSURANCE

The purchase of product liability insurance is actually just one aspect of a corporate function that has recently come to be known as risk management. Risk management involves four basic functions:

1. Identification of risks. These are the threats to the earnings of the firm and its people that may derive from malfunction of a product or process or from a product's failure to perform.* For example, when the Cox, Sabin, and Salk vaccines were first developed, the doctors and biochemists identified the major risks as coming from (a) failure of the product to protect an inoculated child; (b) the vaccine itself causing polio; (c) the product causing temporary side effects but giving protection; (d) the product causing temporary side effects but giving no protection; (e) the product protecting or not protecting, but causing permanent side effects. A host of other possibilities need not encumber us here.

2. Evaluation of risks. What degree of threat does it pose? Continuing the vaccine example: Biostatisticians estimated that paralytic polio would be vaccine-caused in roughly one case per million doses. Each case would have a verdict range of $500 to $600,000, with exposure shared by three companies. Profits on all these doses were, as one official put it, "peanuts." The risks were far too high for even an equitable profit picture.

3. Elimination or minimization of risks by all practical loss-control procedures and equipment. Here the reader is referred back to the discussion of the five areas of manufacturer negligence (pp. 45–52) and to the next chapter, which deals with liability prevention. Work closely with your insurer if he has a loss-control group or with any company that might be covering you under their vendor's endorsement. The larger manufacturers have been building up impressive loss-control capabilities, and if one of them is covering you, he might be willing to provide the services quite reasonably and efficiently.

In the vaccine example, extreme precautions were taken, and the purity of the products eventually surpassed initial predictions.

4. Acceptance, funding, or transfer of the risks. As has been alluded to already, a company may accept all risks (non-insure), establish funding to cover some risks, and/or transfer risk to an

---

* We recognize that risks also come from fire, explosion, accidents, injuries, loss of earnings, and so forth, but our focus here is on product liability.

insurance carrier. In this chapter we will discuss some methods for accomplishing each of these.

In the vaccine example, the company managements transferred the risks by having the federal government assume responsibility for all effects—making the government an insurer which took on the responsibility in recognition of the public services being rendered.

The Risk Manager

Once a risk management function has been established in a company, an experienced product liability insurance person should be appointed for this position. He or she should be an executive with the ability to communicate directly with top management —indeed, report directly to it—and the ability to speak the language of engineering, sales, financial, and production personnel. While the risk manager works for a profit-making organization, which does have to get a product sold, he must not be hindered if he calls attention to an exposure to litigation that might be beyond the capabilities or willingness of insurers to accept. He may even have to press for the withdrawal of certain products from the market. His relationships with sales personnel may turn sour in cases where a nebulous product advantage is being "puffed" to keep up with competition and cover certain application shortcomings, and he calls a halt.

The manager's frame of reference must be broad. He deals with highly conflicting interests, both within the company and outside it. Consider the situation within the company: Legal people would tend to eliminate all possible exposure and virtually put the company out of business. Sales people tend to stress taking a risk to make a sale or beat competition. Technical people would build the 100 percent safe mousetrap—at a price no one could afford to pay. Meanwhile, top management wants the widest spread between revenues and costs. The position of risk manager must, therefore, be structured so that he does not report to any of the functionally conflicting interests, and yet works within the guidelines set up by top management. His views should be sought and carefully considered by the rest of the organization with respect to labeling and other precautionary advice involving the safe use of a product.

Many small companies will not be able to afford this position and the attendant overhead. If this is the case, risk management should be made part of the job description of an existing position, turned over to a retained consultant, or partially shifted to a risk manager employed by a trade association. In all of these cases, we would suggest that the risk manager be responsible for continuously applying the basic steps of risk management—identification, evaluation, elimination, and (usually) transfer. The manager's performance should be judged by how well he or she performs these steps. It should also be measured by how well the coverage gaps have been closed and the purchase of insurance coverage carried out.

Insurance Options

If your company is large enough or is associated with an industrial group, it is usually its own insurer—except for catastrophic dollar loss situations. The definition of "catastrophic" varies with the size of the company. For an auto industry giant it would be an astronomical figure; for a small manufacturer it would be quite modest.

If your company has sufficient spread of risk, it might have the prerequisites for starting an insurance firm of its own—known today as a captive insurance firm. This device frequently offers broader coverage, lower costs, and other favorable conditions, provided it is properly backed up by several forms of reinsurance against catastrophe.

If your company is too small to qualify for such a venture it may profit by joining an industrial association, in which case the options for possible action include the following:

1. *Recommended insurance firm.* This is the first and possibly the simplest of several alternatives for an association. After careful negotiation with a few selected insurance firms, one would be selected whose costs, forms of coverage, and reputation for handling claims would best serve the membership. Each member would then negotiate with that carrier, either directly

or through a broker of its own choice. Members could obtain additional negotiating help from outside consulting services.

2. *Mass marketing.* This is similar to the above but requires joint negotiation by a representative body of the membership. Individual policies are still written for the members at a discount reflecting the reduced broker or agency costs.

3. *Industrial group policy.* This differs from the foregoing in that a single policy is written for all the subscribing members, with the loss experience and premiums pooled in a single account with one or more insurance carriers. The association acts as the policy holder and issues certificates of coverage, with full details, to the various members. The amount of coverage, the deductibles, the costs, and so forth are adjusted to the needs of each member and so noted on each certificate of coverage. In this plan, all premiums are funneled through the association or its designee to the insurer. Claims administration requires close cooperation with and assistance from the member companies, as claims too pass through the association or its designee to the insurer.

4. *Industrial group policy overriding existing coverage.* This is similar to the foregoing but is essentially a high-level policy intended to broaden the basic coverage along the lines of "umbrella" policies which have been in force for several years. Such a policy, tailored by the association, could include many forms of coverage that are not now available or that have been found to be inadequate.

5. *Mutual or trust fund.* Such coverage will become essentially a service contract, particularly if the no-fault concept extends from the automobile arena into product liability, as it well might do in the next few years. An industry that is planning on a long-range basis can obtain great economies, better coverage, and other significant advantages through collective funding of some kind. There are many types available; all that is needed to set up a mutual fund is sufficient members who are willing to pool their interests.

6. *An industry captive insurance firm.* One of the most effective ways to develop and control the sources and costs of insurance, including product liability insurance, is the ownership of a

captive insurance firm. We refer here to one designed to serve members of an industrial association rather than the public. Such a firm provides long-term, stabilized insurance capacity on essentially a cost-plus basis, and could be very beneficial to members in controlling product liability claims.

Once the firm has established an operating plan to determine its "net retention" and the top limits of coverage required by its members, it would seek reinsurance both here and abroad, so as to respond effectively to claims and protect its capital structure.

7. *Standby bank credit.* Several of the leading banks are prepared to offer standby credit for a modest fee plus current interest rates. They offer a ten-year payback period with limits high enough to protect a fund or captive insurance firm.

THE INSURANCE PURCHASE

The risk management function in the company will generally be charged with responsibility for all contacts between the company and the insurance brokers or underwriters, unless special arrangements have been drawn up between management and retained counsel with respect to potential or actual claims. Thus, as noted earlier, a major responsibility involved in risk management is the actual purchase of insurance coverage.

One must understand that in negotiating insurance, the manufacturer is not really a buyer and the insurer is not really a seller. Quite to the contrary, the insured is in the position of a seller of risk to the underwriter. He must be prepared to share this risk in the form of deductibles and occasionally a portion of the risk above the deductibles—as well as, of course, any losses which exceed the limits of his policy. It is not the purpose of this chapter to decide the size of the deductibles applicable to any particular industry, the top limits of coverage that might be desirable, or methods for sharing the loss experience with the insurance industry. Consultants are available to do this for those companies which do not have sufficiently experienced or trained risk managers on their staff or access to them through a trade association or vendor-company arrangements.

The purchase of insurance is as much a specialty function as the management of cash reserves in a company. As mentioned earlier, if no risk manager position per se exists, its de facto existence should nevertheless be acknowledged, and the person who makes decisions in this area must invest the time, ·effort, and study necessary to the task.

The risk manager may be assisted by a broker, an agent, or an outside consultant operating on a fee basis. Fundamentally, he must do whatever is necessary to protect the assets, earning power, and personnel of his company, particularly against the catastrophic loss. It is best to have catastrophe insurance that is complete in all respects, even with a higher deductible than one would normally be inclined to accept. All loopholes and gaps in coverage should be properly plugged. It is not the losses that can be covered out of earnings or borrowings which are of prime concern, but rather the thalidomide type of tragedy which requires enormous financial backup.

The remainder of this section is addressed to the risk manager. There are many considerations leading to the best purchase decision, some obviously interrelated. The following guidelines are by no means complete, but are nevertheless offered here in the hope that they will aid you in your purchase decision making and help you to audit the decision processes already in use.

Step 1. Estimate what you can easily absorb without any coverage at all. Be careful to include amounts for legal fees in addition to settlement values. Include provisions for absorbing overhead costs for engineers, production personnel, and others who may be brought into an accident investigation. In small suits, your legal fees may exceed the claim payout by a huge amount.

Next estimate what you can put into an investment fund, its payouts, its replenishment, and all the aspects of running an in-house insurance operation. The remainder of your exposure will be covered through some form of risk transfer.

Step 2. Open direct communications with the underwriters

who handle product liability insurance. Sometimes, particularly if your firm is small, you; will not be able to interest an insurance underwriter in directly handling your account. Then you will be obliged to deal with a broker or agent.

Many of the direct-writing insurance firms are deeply involved in loss-prevention activities and in developing expertise. They can send loss-prevention teams into your plant to evaluate product safety and provide other loss-control activities—which gives you additional reason for working with them directly. In some industries, or for some types of products, you will find an attitude of disinterest on the part of insurance firms when it comes to extending product liability coverage. If you are not big enough to offer substantial premiums for comprehensive coverage and other coverage a business needs, they may rebuff your attempts to obtain coverage for product liability. Here you may want to work through your trade association, as noted previously.

Step 3. Consult with your legal, insurance, field service, sales, and engineering people, plus all other parties who can contribute to a detailed analysis of your past loss experience. Include those claims you absorbed by deductibles or non-insurance as well as those which were referred to and paid by a carrier.

After analyzing your own claim experience, search for more data which might indicate future trends. Contact firms in the insurance industry for access to their loss records. There is a vast body of information that you should be able to tap when you meet with these underwriters and begin discussing the coverage you might need.

Often the risk manager will find he is the first person in his company to have sought such information. This is illustrated by the experience of one risk manager: After having estimated realistically the loss potential on main incoming plant transformers, he tried to persuade the chief engineer to separate two such units by a fire wall or by sufficient distance so that if one blew it would not take out the other one as well. The engineer rejected the suggestion, stating that in all his years of experience he had rarely heard of such a transformer exploding or catching fire. The risk manager then went, quietly, to the insurance industry files and found a long list of losses involving this type of equipment. When he presented these data to the chief engineer, it became obvious that the engineer had never possessed the information he needed to make an intelligent decision—that information having been "hidden away" in insurance firm files. In no time the transformers were properly protected, and a completely new attitude toward loss evaluation and control spread through the entire company.

Many types of barriers and filters exist that can deprive the decision maker of the basic information input he needs. This is true whether the decision maker be a draftsman, an engineer, a sales person, a division manager, or top management.

There are several barriers that may exist in the decision maker's own mind. First, most decision makers do not know of the insurance firms' files or just never think of them as a source of information. Second, most of them consider insurance as outside their scope of responsibilities or concerns, and consequently have had no working experience with insurance firms. Third, many of them know nothing about the intricacies of insurance, and therefore show a common organizational-behavior pattern in turning away from an "unknown" even it if could supply needed data.

Even the risk manager himself may throw up a barrier. He may confine his attention solely to insurance questions—from fire to theft to workmen's compensation—and not have a working relationship with departments that could use him as a key to unlock information sources.

Sometimes information is "filtered" (censored) before it can reach the decision maker. The filters which hinder the decision maker operate on three levels. The first of these is the reluctance on the part of equipment salesmen (e.g., the transformer salesman) to advise a potential buyer that the equipment could break down and therefore ought to be protected by spare equipment and physical safeguarding. This is not good salesmanship.

The second filter may be found in the service or repair department of an equipment manufacturer, where the actual breakdowns and failures are well recognized (and usually corrected). Top management is reluctant to allow service departments to advise sales of these difficulties, on the grounds that sales personnel must remain "optimists."

The third filter is the insurance industry, which usually pays the losses for all types of equipment manufacturers and users and thus has a body of information which would be valuable to the decision maker mentioned above. So far, most insurance companies have refused to release such information. In the opinion of the authors, the information should be made available in a form that will preserve ethical anonymity while providing working facts and figures to promote product safety.

Another place to obtain loss or claims information, particularly where the insurance industry does not provide proper breakdowns or analyses, is the trade association itself. Of course, here one runs into another filter: the understandable organizational reluctance to pry into the affairs of its various members, who in turn are reluctant to reveal what they might consider competitive data. It is possible, however, to convince most members that this data, assembled anonymously, does not give the next company a competitive edge and that the assembled information will help everyone.

Besides using insurance industry data, a risk manager may also be able, on occasion, to tap the knowledge of other risk managers in his industry. They may be able to supply information not only on claims but also on costs of coverage, levels of deductibles, and favorable terms and conditions in the various contracts. This sharing of information, which is a good method to determine whether or not your program is in line with the best available, requires good faith among risk managers. Obviously, attendance at seminars, conferences, and group meetings will build the bridges to such information.

Step 4. Assemble all endorsements and supplementary correspondence pertaining to your existing policies lest some cutbacks or changes in coverage of which you have been notified become mislaid. Next, examine the policies carefully and take steps to amend them if necessary. Check whether the named insured in the policy is broad enough to include the parent company, its separate divisions, subsidiaries, and affiliates, and other entities for which product liability coverage is desired—including automatic coverage (with a reasonable period for notifying the carrier) for new acquisitions or mergers. The standard policy, as previously discussed, may have territorial limitations. Seek endorsements to broaden this coverage accordingly. The basic coverage usually includes bodily injury and property damage. Bodily injury should be broadened to "personal injury," which would include libel, slander, false arrest, and other charges as well as punitive damages.* This, too, can be done by endorsement.

Wherever the phrase "caused by accident" appears, it should be changed to "caused by occurrence." Incidentally, new policies define "occurrence" as an "accident" but, in addition, enlarge the definition to include "exposure to conditions which may continue over an indefinite period of time." Some underwriters will substitute the word "occurrence" for "accident" when so requested.

Many vendors and dealers request that the manufacturer's policy be extended to include them. When so endorsed, the policy usually covers only the contingent legal liability of the vendor arising out of the acts of the manufacturer. Unless a special endorsement is written, it will not cover negligence by the vendor himself. If a manufacturer advises the vendor that he is covered and this is not so, the vendor may then have a right to hold the manufacturer responsible largely because of this reassurance. It is recommended, therefore, that you carefully examine all endorsements for vendors to determine whether or not the vendor's own negligence is covered and reconsider whether or not it should be.

With respect to the liability of others assumed under contract, the standard policy covers ordinary contracts such as railroad sidetrack agreements † but does not cover hold-harmless agreements between a manufacturer and a general contractor, a builder, or other party unless specifically recognized and endorsed on the product liability or general liability policy. There

---

* In one case a California jury brought a $21.7 million verdict against the defendant, of which $17.5 million was punitive damages.[6]

† These are agreements in which railroads providing track service into a shipper's plant make him assume all liability, even if the locomotive starts a fire in the plant and the fire spreads to other firms' buildings.

is, however, an endorsement known as "blanket contractual" which provides automatic coverage of many contracts. These contracts must be reported periodically to the insurer.

Recall insurance, as noted earlier in this chapter, has to be specifically endorsed to the product liability policy or written completely independently. Such coverage is now difficult to obtain and may require the assistance of consultants, who can set up captive insurance companies, work out single policies for associations, and so forth.

It is recommended that all forms of liability coverage—general, automobile, workmen's compensation, etc., as well as product liability—be placed with the same insurance carrier in order to avoid one carrier passing the buck to another through subrogation actions. On major machinery installations, it is frequently possible to provide a "wrap-up policy" in which the same insurance carrier is responsible for "completed operations" and for product liability arising from the operations of all contractors, subcontractors, component parts suppliers, and others who might contribute directly or indirectly to a serious incident. This coverage can be negotiated. Completed-operations coverage insures against damages that result from a faulty installation after the contractor has completed his work and it has been accepted by the owner or abandoned by the contractor.[7]

The whole question of product liability arising from design, formula, plans, specifications, advertising material, printed instructions, etc., is subject to amendment and negotiation with your carrier. There are gaps between a product liability policy and another form of insurance known as "errors and omissions" insurance. There are other gaps between these two and the "officers and directors liability" policy. Rather than providing a checklist for all these pieces of protection, we simply recommend that you negotiate a special umbrella policy to cover all design, manufacturing, sales, and distribution activities on the broadest possible basis. Obtain high limits, while sacrificing, if necessary, coverage for the smaller losses under an appropriate deductible. The insurance plan should cover not only the mistakes, errors, and omissions of executives and selected middle managers, but those of all managers, all group and section leaders, and all first-line supervisors.[8] This is no place to save on overhead; covering these individuals protects you, protects them,* and also makes them feel part of the company in every way.

Step 5. Demonstrate your existing product-liability-prevention program to the insurer, as well as your plans for the future. A program is outlined more fully in the next chapter. Here, we will just point out that your efforts, directives, testing, design practices, and procedures must be documented. Insurers are particularly worried about design errors. Be careful, therefore, to illustrate how your engineers perform fault analyses, fail-safe analyses, and all other applicable techniques to insure a safe product.

Step 6. Review your policies and endorsements again, this time consulting with knowledgeable people inside and outside your organization. Make absolutely sure there are no gaps in the coverage you need.

Step 7. Allocate the company's insurance dollars to buy the protection you need—whether it's fire, theft, workmen's compensation, or product liability coverage. Allocate funds for loss-prevention activities to demonstrate your continuing concern for product safety, including beefing up quality control, adding to the company's field service capability, or simply training salesmen to be more careful about what they claim your product can do and to be sure to reveal its limitations or dangers. Remember that risk management includes minimizing or eliminating risk situations. This cannot be left solely in the hands of the busy executive, whose performance will be judged on how many units he can ship out the door on any given day, or to the salesman, whose performance will be judged by the dollar volume of sales.

---

* Malone says a court might hold an engineer or inspector personally liable if he sees a dangerous condition developing and does not stop the work when he could have exercised discretion and done so. In a case involving a construction job the employer was held liable, but the language of the decision could easily be extended to cover managers, leaders, and supervisors in all industries.[9]

IN SUMMARY

We have by no means covered all the intricate details of product liability insurance, or, for that matter, product liability management per se. We hope, however, that a person who is familiar with this subject will find the information in this chapter a worthwhile addition to his or her knowledge, and that the newcomer will have obtained a reasonably concise grounding in the subject of product liability risk management.

REFERENCES

1. Mark R. Greene, *Risk and Insurance* (Cincinnati: South-Western Publishing Company, 1973), p. 12.
2. Ibid., p. 116.
3. James G. March and Herbert A. Simon, *Organizations* (New York: John Wiley & Sons, 1963), p. 141.
4. Ibid.
5. "Managing the Product Recall," *Business Week* (January 26, 1974), pp. 46–49.
6. "Dangerous Planes," *The Wall Street Journal*, July 30, 1971, p. 1.
7. Greene, op. cit., p. 340.
8. George A. Peters, "Quality and the Law: Reactions to Liability," *Quality Management and Engineering* (March 1971), p. 30; and George A. Peters, "Quality and the Law: Your Personal Liability," *Quality Assurance* (February 1971), p. 28.
9. Edward E. Malone, "The Power to 'Stop the Work': A Serious Source of Potential Liability," *Consulting Engineer* (June 1971), pp. 24, 26.

6

PRODUCT
LIABILITY
PREVENTION

Until now, our major concern has been legal and insurance defenses against product liability suits. We have included in our coverage a number of learning experiences for future decision making. In this chapter we will examine a more positive approach—namely, liability prevention—which forestalls the need to call on your insurer or be involved in litigation. It is possible to keep the liability problem within bounds and, indeed, to reduce it to truly insignificant proportions.

OTHER BENEFITS OF PRODUCT SAFETY

We do not overlook the fact that the sum total of our recommendations will appreciably add to your overhead costs, so you may not choose to carry out all of them. The ultra-safe product encompassing the engineering dreamworld would provide the best form of liability prevention, but it probably would bankrupt the company. Of the recommendations given in this chapter, you should pick and choose only the ones you really need. However, when you draw the boundaries of your program, consider that product safety efforts have benefits transcending the issue of liability. These benefits are in three major areas: compliance with CPSC regulations, compliance with OSHA, and protection of your company's reputation.

The Consumer Product Safety Commission

By working to improve product safety, you will be accommodating yourself to the intent and ever broadening scope of this agency. The Commission was created in 1972 and was a direct outgrowth of the findings and recommendations of the National Commission on Product Safety [1] and two years of congressional hearings and deliberations. The Commission is a five-member regulatory body appointed by the President and confirmed by the Senate. It operates independently of any other executive department and has jurisdiction over those products offered for sale for the personal use, consumption, or enjoyment of consumers in residential, recreational, or institutional environments with the exception of those products previously under federal regulation.*

William White, acting director of CPSC's Bureau of Information and Education, has written a good summary of the Commission's powers. The CPSC is empowered to:

1. Collect, analyze, and disseminate relevant injury and hazard data.
2. Conduct product safety investigations.
3. Test products and develop test methods.
4. Develop standards governing a variety of product characteristics.
5. Inform consumers of product hazards.
6. Ban products found to be unreasonably hazardous and not susceptible to any feasible safety standard.
7. Classify, ban, and seize imminently hazardous products.
8. Require marketing notice and descriptions of new products.
9. Require certification that a product complies with the ap-

---

* Namely, motor vehicles, tobacco, certain poisons, boats, foods, drugs, cosmetics, and radiation products.

propriate standard, plus identification of its date and place of production and its manufacturer.

10. Require manufacturers, distributors, or retailers to give public notice of deficient products (i.e., those products that fail to meet applicable standards or contain substantially hazardous defects).

11. Require manufacturers, distributors, or retailers of deficient products to:
    (a) bring the product into conformance or
    (b) replace it with one meeting the applicable standard, free of charge to the consumer, or
    (c) refund the purchase price.

12. Inspect manufacturing plants, warehouses, or conveyances at reasonable times and only in product safety related areas.

13. Require record-keeping by manufacturers, labelers, or distributors of data the Commission considers necessary for implementation of the Act. These records must be available for Commission inspection.

14. Refuse admission to, test, seize, and destroy deficient imported products.

15. Subpoena records, documents, or witnesses.

16. Conduct hearings; file and litigate suits; issue formal notices of noncompliance.

17. Obtain free samples of imported consumer products where necessary and purchase at cost any domestically produced consumer product.

18. Construct and operate research and testing facilities.

19. Establish a Product Safety Advisory Council composed of five members each from consumer groups, governmental agencies, and consumer product industries.

20. Establish federal-state cooperative programs.[2]

Some of the functions previously carried out by other government agencies now fall under the CPSC. These include:

From the Department of Health, Education and Welfare (HEW): the Hazardous Substances Act, the Toy Safety and Children Protection Act, and portions of the Flammable Fabrics Act. From the Department of Commerce (DOC) and the Federal Trade Commission (FTC): remaining portions of the Flammable Fabrics Act (except flammability research and testing being conducted by DOC's National Bureau of Standards) and those portions of the Federal Trade Commission Act which relate to implementation of the Flammable Fabrics Act. From FTC: the Refrigerator Safety Act. From HEW and the Environmental Protection Agency (EPA): the Poison Prevention Packaging Act (PPPA). . . .

Under the PPPA, safety closure regulations have been promulgated for aspirin containers, liquid furniture polish, methyl salicylate, addictive drugs, lye preparations, turpentine, methyl alcohol, sulfuric acid, illuminating and kindling preparations, and oral prescription drugs except nitroglycerin. Another nine categories of products are being actively considered for closure regulations.[3]

Section 15b of the Consumer Product Safety Act has become the major focus of the Commission.[4] It requires the manufacturer or others in the stream of commerce to report within 24 hours the detection of the existence of a substantial hazard. The Commission demands retrofits, recalls, public warnings, and reimbursements to buyers. Thus it becomes expensive indeed to put out an unsafe product or to fail to comply with federal safety standards.

On the issue of product liability suits, we again quote William White: "Compliance with federal safety standards does not guarantee immunity from liability, but it certainly will help."[5]

The Occupational Safety and Health Act

By improving product safety you will also be accommodating yourself to the intent and purposes of the Occupational Safety and Health Act (OSHA)[6] if you sell your products to industrial or commercial users.

The Act's regulations—which cover industry, construction, and maritime employers—encompass close to 500 Federal Register pages.[7] The provisions of OSHA permit workers to become involved in both the administrative and enforcement aspects of the Act. In a 1973 article,[8] Senator Harrison Williams, Jr., a co-author of the Act, succinctly summed up what he termed "the workers' environmental bill of rights":

1. Right to observe the monitoring of harmful substances and to have access to records of monitoring.
2. Right to request OSHA to perform a special inspection.
3. Right to have a representative accompany an OSHA inspector.
4. Right to have all citations posted so that employees will know of any violations found by an inspector.
5. Right to obtain review within Labor Department if inspector fails to issue a citation after employees have provided written statement of alleged violations.
6. Right to appeal to OSHRC * if it is believed [that the] time given to abate violation is unreasonably long. Right to oppose any appeal taken by an employer to the OSHRC.
7. Right to participate in standards-setting process by offering evidence and comments on proposed standards.
8. Right to appeal to United States Court of Appeals on grounds that Secretary's action in setting a standard is not based on substantial evidence.
9. Right to obtain a hearing on employer's request for a variance to a standard.
10. Right to request the Department of Health, Education and Welfare to determine whether substances found in the workplace are toxic.
11. Right to have Secretary of Labor seek redress if an employee has been discriminated against for exercising rights under the Act.
12. Right to be represented in a mandamus † action to require Secretary of Labor to abate an imminent danger.

As you help your customer provide a safe workplace, you will directly benefit yourself. Provisions 1 and 4 above have enhanced the climate for subrogation actions against you when your customer's employees are injured. This happens in one of two ways:

1. The employee collects workmen's compensation insurance. The insurer, in turn, sues the tool builder, chemical supplier, or equipment manufacturer in a subrogation action to

---

* OSHRC stands for the Occupational Safety and Health Review Commission—the quasi-judicial arm of OSHA.

† A mandamus is a judicial order commanding performance by a public officer of a specific act or duty.

recover his payout. Thus, in this type of subrogation action, insurer A sues supplier B to recover payments made for injuries to C.

2. The employee collects workmen's compensation insurance but then enters suit against the builder, supplier, etc., on his own. If he collects damages, those damages will be distributed between the employee himself and the employee's insurer, with the insurer being reimbursed up to the full amount it paid the employee. Of course, if the damages awarded exceed the amount the employee collected from the insurer, the employee receives the remainder. (The intent here is to prevent an injured party from collecting twice—once in payments and once by a judicial award—for the same injury.) In this situation the insurer's subrogation action is embedded in the employee's suit.

In some lines of insurance, particularly liability, recoveries from negligent parties through subrogation are substantial. Whether the subrogation is from the insurer alone or through the employee's suit, the target is still the "deep pocket" suppliers to the employer.

OSHA is fostering new research into long-recognized industrial noise, shock, and vibration hazards. As new findings emerge from the laboratories on the harmful effects of long-term exposure to existing levels, liability suits will be generated. As noted earlier, compliance with a federal standard is not a guarantee against liability. Hearing loss and noise provide a good illustration of what we mean:

Some researchers put the maximum noise level to which people can be exposed without hearing damage at 55 decibels (a noisy office) over an eight-hour day. A level of 85 decibels results in hearing damage without warning; that is, there is no pain sensation felt by the average person. OSHA permits an eight-hour exposure of 90 decibels—a level known to be risky. (OSHA balanced the economic costs of making the workplace quieter against the possible damage from noise and opted for the noise as not really doing "that much damage.") The manufacturer who wants to protect himself against future liability claims related to hearing loss should aim not at OSHA regulations but at what researchers recognize as a truly safe noise level.

Reputation

Finally, consider the value of avoiding blots on your company's reputation. Your product will be compared with others in the increasing proliferation of consumer publications. If a competitor develops a safer product, it will be compared by name with yours, and buyers will learn about the innovator's better quality.

Whether your advertising is specific or not, the Federal Trade Commission is forcing an increasing amount of performance-specification disclosure. Knowledgeable consumers will seek out and use these specifications. The less knowledgeable consumer—who in the past tolerated high levels of uncertainty about product quality—will have considerably less uncertainty if news media connect your trade or company name with a defect, recall, or warning. He will avoid your entire product line in future purchase decisions.[9]

HELP FROM OTHER ORGANIZATIONS

Before we present our extended discussions of how to set up a liability-prevention system within your firm, a few words should be said about external organizations. Two, in particular, can provide very valuable help: the trade association and the independent consultant.

The Trade Association

The firm's risk manager, quality assurance manager, and various engineering groups should work with the trade association for insurance and loss-control purposes. There are a number of ways in which a trade association can help the typical company. It can:

1. Provide consumer education. The association can work through schools and other training agencies to foster more intelligent use of products.
2. Set standards (as we discussed previously).
3. Provide internal education. It can sponsor seminars and product safety publications too expensive for individual members.
4. Supply claims data. The association can gather hazard and risk information, as discussed in Chapter 5.
5. Set up insurance coverage (as was also discussed in Chapter 5).
6. Predict hazards. The association can develop industry-wide design-review and failure-prediction techniques.
7. Educate attorneys. It can help the insurance-industry attorneys defend suits by familiarizing them with design, fabrication, shipping, and quality control techniques used in association members' plants.

In assuming the above roles, however, the trade association must exercise due caution. First, it is important that the association not develop standards, practices, or codes which will amount to a whitewash of the industry at the lowest common denominator of safety. In a product liability case tried before a jury, demonstration that an existing code is simply a shield behind which even the weakest manufacturer can hide is frequently more damaging than no code at all. Second, the association must not be pushed into acting in an obstructionist role regarding new government safety requirements. Third, the association should not allow its integrity to be impeached, regardless of the size of the suborner. A company which drops out of a highly respected trade group will find that fact used against it in a lawsuit. While this is a negative way to build membership, it is a positive way to promote good ethics.

The Independent Consultant

The independent consultant to the corporation acts as an independent auditor of the product safety, quality, and reliability in much the same manner that a public accounting firm audits the firm's books. The maintenance of such an independent auditor would go far to convince a jury in a liability case of the sincerity of the firm in its wish to produce only the safest products. Without any allegiance to any particular group within the firm, this auditor would be able to accomplish the following: (1) Could independently audit decision-making processes, design reviews, instructions, maintenance manuals, and conformance to up-to-date practices in product liability prevention. (2) Could independently review the management information system to see to it that the quality of the information that reaches management is high, accurately reflects relevant issues in liability prevention, is formatted to highlight the important information, and furthers the management's profit, safety, and growth aims. (3) Could provide aid in the expert witness category and help during lawsuit preparation.

INTRODUCTION: DEVELOPING A SYSTEM FOR LIABILITY PREVENTION

Our discussion of a system for liability prevention is most easily presented in two parts. The first will focus on liability-prevention documentation, or the "building blocks" of the system. These yield, in toto, the written plan—including objectives, policies, and procedures—for your company's loss-control and hazard-elimination efforts.

Our building blocks include three major sets of documents that guide the product-related decision making of company personnel, three major sets of documents that serve to audit their decision and physical outputs, and one set of documents that establishes the all-important system for tracing product genealogy. We will not concern ourselves here with those documents which, while playing some role in liability prevention, are already incorporated in most firms' standard-operations guides.

The second part of our discussion will go into program administration. This we divide into five major areas, namely:

1. The roles of top management and of the liability-prevention administrator.
2. The function of a design-review team.
3. The roles of various departments in implementing liability prevention in the firm.
4. Implementation of liability prevention throughout the product's life cycle.
5. Some pointers on the operation of a liability defense team.

DOCUMENTATION

With rapid organizational changes and a normal personnel turnover, documents may be the only proof you have that you did indeed design to the state of the art, properly construct, and so forth, should litigation involve one of your products. We group the various types of documents into three major categories: performance, audit, and genealogy.

Performance Documents

The "performance" category includes, first, in-house guideline documents. In format these are manuals designed to assure that every product, at every step in bringing it to market, is properly accompanied by appropriate written material. Second are checklists which are designed for use at the workplace to assure against leaving out critical parts, labels, instructions, or shipping materials. Third are documents relating to external relations: documents setting forth special public relations standby procedures to reduce the negative impact of product deficiencies, and documents that control vendor and customer contractual relationships.

Guideline documents
We will discuss six major manuals that should be in use. These internal working documents control the paperwork for liability prevention in regard to specific products.

A specification content and format guideline manual. This is the basic manual which controls how company products are described—from inception through sales, service, and disposition. This manual tells what terminology to use in describing the product, how to write a general description, and how to write up product characteristics so that all functions in the firm will know what has to be designed, tested, and so forth. In firms that do not have such a manual, one product (which might be the pet of the chief engineer) will have a tome listing every detail of its performance, safety, and other properties; another product will have a three-sentence description. With the latter product, each organizational function will attribute to the product whatever characteristics it feels are pertinent. In such cases it is not unusual to find, in court, that two different departments in the firm had two widely varying conceptions of what the product was able or was supposed to do.

Format is also very important and must be controlled. Some firms use printed forms to assure that all characteristics and performance requirements are entered in a uniform and complete manner.

A drafting-standards manual. This manual usually contains one or more applicable national standards from a trade or professional organization plus standards particular to the firm's own needs. As the product moves onto the drawing board, we are concerned with pass-along-information problems. The engineers have the prototype; the draftsmen have to put it on paper. The drafting manual must specify that safety items are to be shown in a specific, clearly identified manner and that all safety features of the prototype must be incorporated in the production model.

The draftsman's product is the sheet of paper from which all production follows. It must be complete to insure that unwise substitutions of parts or components cannot be made at some point during production. A complete drawing, showing all safety items, helps provide the firm with a defense against a charge of design error should one or more of the items be accidentally left off the product during production. In view of the seriousness of design error, from both insurance and product-recall aspects, the complete drawing is a formidable aid to defense. A drafting-standards manual helps assure that the drawing contains all pertinent features.

The drawing checkers must have the manual to guide them in their work—especially to catch omissions in product details. You should assume that anything not shown in the drawing will be furnished during production by the least-informed persons around. If you guard against this happening, you protect against possible challenges to your product.

A workmanship-standards manual. Workmanship standards are generally prepared by quality assurance personnel and coordinated with engineering and manufacturing. Watch out for standards established and never attained in your shop. Bring up the shop level or make the standard realistic, but don't be in violation of your own rules.

The workmanship-standards manual should tell how to set these standards and how to determine whether standards are realistic. It gives instructions for formulating detailed documents on everything from tolerances not specified in drawings to the checklist the packers should use to make sure every product has instructions, warranties, and cautions in the box before shipping. The manual should require that every product have its own set of fabrication and assembly procedures, even if the procedures appear to be carbon copies of those used on earlier products. There should be a close tie between the date the model of a particular product went into production and the date of the documents; you have weakened yourself if your attorney must use "old" documents to defend you against charges of negligence in construction.

A safety code manual. This is based on safety standards, codes, and practices for the product in question. Four primary sources for these items are: [10]

The government (e.g., rules and regulations established by the Consumer Product Safety Commission and FDA).

Industry and trade associations (whose information is gleaned from industry practices).

Individual concerns, which create standards in fulfilling

customer (particularly Department of Defense) contracts or establish standards through general use.

Independent sources, which develop them on the basis of safety principles and trade usage.

Standards, codes, and practices from any of these sources are admissible as evidence in many courts.[11] They have particular impact on a jury when a contract incorporates the standards.

The safety code manual should be a regularly updated looseleaf that incorporates the outputs of all four sources and indexes them in such fashion that they are readily available to everyone. This manual is sometimes a part of the firm's design manual, but when this is done, personnel from production, advertising, and other departments shy away from using it.

A good computerized index has obvious advantages. Foreign markets, in particular, require performance to specialized standards and certification of this performance by laboratories designated by the importing country's government. Specifying that the product must meet the standards (as opposed to presenting a series of test requirements) is the most flexible and least costly way of handling most export-certification problems. The effects of wear and tear should be specified, and all persons should be alerted to try to eliminate features that contribute marginal gains to product performance at some cost in safety.

A manual of change-control procedures. Callbacks and disasters are caused when changes made on drawings are not incorporated in the finished production item. A large commercial transport crashed because of a faulty cargo door; a production change had not been incorporated on this aircraft even though it had left the factory with the change notice signed off.[12] The courts have held that it is a continuous duty of the manufacturer to improve his product, particularly when its safety has been questioned. The insurance company will enforce this requirement, as we have previously discussed.

The change-control-procedures manual tells how to put through a change and make sure it gets onto the product before it leaves the plant. The manual may incorporate simple field retrofit procedures, or it may establish a full set of procedures which insure that field service personnel are notified of a problem, are trained in its rectification, are supplied with tools and materials for accomplishing tasks, and are required to report back through a feedback system that keeps tight control over what has and has not been retrofitted.

Design modifications usually generate most of the change problems. Keeping track of them, especially when trying to meet the differing needs of customers, will often result in the loss of crucial change information or even of basic safety features. McDonald [13] suggests focusing on a master parts list (MPL) which provides an organized and coded file of every part and assembly used in the past on all versions of the particular type of product. In his change-control system, McDonald lists for each part all the information normally found in a bill of materials. But the basic reference structure by which the system is accessed is the MPL, which has three levels of items:

> The interchangeable components of finished products.
> The first subdivisions of each component (called the "options"). The options comprise a list of parts of a machine performing a function, all of which would be removed if the function were deleted.
> Low-level subassemblies in the options.

All of this is computerized and coded (indexed) for easy reference. Its use for our purposes becomes self-evident: A customer ordering a specific option would find that according to the MPL it will be supplied only with a specific safety device—or not at all.

A manual of engineering test procedures. The product must be able to do what it is supposed to do and withstand foreseeable abuse. This procedures manual makes sure that a test document is drawn up for each product and prescribes the intent or type of tests to be performed. The details applicable to each product are then filled in on the product test document. This document is updated by engineering, legal, and risk management functions in the firm. Whenever a product abuse surfaces and a testing procedure can predetermine what the effect of this abuse will be, the manual can call for the test to be applied to all future products. It is necessary to require tests that show up defects under cumulative stresses. If the product is to sustain vibration at high altitudes, testing procedures should not accept first a ground-level vibration test and later a static exposure to a high-altitude chamber.

All the reliability and failure analyses performed on the paper design should be carried out on the "real thing." It is crucial that all records be retained and that all product changes resulting from these tests go through the change-control procedure.

We have not included managerial operations manuals, design manuals, and other manuals we have seen in most firms—of which there is a virtually infinite list. However, those in charge of such manuals—perhaps systems and procedures personnel— may well profit from meeting with their company's attorneys and insurance underwriter loss-control teams to bring their manuals into line with suggestions derived from our material.

Checklists

These types of documents are designed for use at the work site for self-checking by the person performing the work. In format they are a series of checklists which each person—the engineer, designer, assembler, packer, and so forth—uses for sign-off of his or her segment of the production task. Checklists are also valuable instruments as refreshers to sales and field service personnel. With sales personnel, the existence and use of checklists will help provide defense against careless misrepresentation (and creation of a warranty). With field service personnel, checklists help prevent a service being completed without a proper safety check.

Checklists can be grouped for discussion according to whether they are used in design, construction, testing, inspection, or warning.

Design. Design checklists should encompass, at the minimum, checkoff points for the following:

Completeness and accuracy of system or product specifications.

Completeness and accuracy of block diagrams for system or product.

Applicable safety standards.

Applicable human-engineering safety devices. Checklists should cover the effects of removal of the devices, the effects of failure of the devices, and methods for checking that the devices remain operative during the life of the product.

Adequacy of design reviews for fail-safe operation. (Design review will be covered later.)

Accuracy and thoroughness of reports of failures in development, and documentation bearing on the choice of final design.

Accuracy of computations.

Accuracy of drawings, including material and construction specifications.

Checklists for individual firms will, of course, contain items peculiar to their products, as well as items gleaned from litigation results and field service reports.

Construction. This area encompasses the very broad gamut of operations from raw-materials purchase to shipping and may require up to a half dozen or so individual departmental lists.

Materials procurement, which may also be responsible for all inventories, should include checking:

Purchase-order specifications.

Incoming inspection or vendor-premises inspection.

Damage reports.

Incoming packaging deficiencies.

Materials-substitution approvals (to be obtained from design engineering).

Shelf life, utilization, and storage of stock.

Materials' performance and suitability for manufacturing needs.

Replacement of rejected parts and disposal of the latter.

Replacing nonperforming vendors or vendors of poor-quality components.

The manufacturing function must guard against human errors through timely inspections and must prevent improper substitution of materials or components to achieve production targets. Items passing through manufacturing should have:

Proper lot, batch, production-run, or other identification numbers.

Proper documentation as to change orders implemented, drawings followed, and procedures that governed assembly.

Acceptance by quality control as conforming to written specifications and all standards in methods and materials.

Signed approval of rework procedures performed on any items.

All test readings taken during inspections (if applicable).

Additional check items that will serve to prove an entire shipment was made in the same way and from the same components or materials as the samples which passed inspection.

A check for proper application of all labels and precautionary notices.

A check that all workmanship standards have been met.

Testing. Product testing may be done in two stages during its life cycle. Testing seeks to determine: Does the product perform as it was intended to perform and fail only in a safe manner in all foreseeable situations? The answer is sought first by testing hand-built prototypes and then by testing samples from the first production run. Some firms test new products by lending or giving first-production-run samples to employees of geographically dispersed distributors and then carefully monitoring performance.

Checklists for test products must be extremely carefully tailored, but we suggest looking for, at the least:

Documentation as to tests of hand-built prototypes and conditions of these tests.

Documentation of all failures of prototypes, justification and approval of all design changes, and retest results with redesigned prototypes.

Documentation of all differences (and justification therefor) between prototypes and production run.

Location, environmental conditions, and other use data for every production-unit test.

Proper installation of elapsed time meters or other use-recording devices.

Procedures for complete investigations of failures and re-call of units.

Field test of installation and use instructions.

Packaging and shipping will often create problems that may later be attributed to prior steps in the product life cycle. Instruction sheets may be left out of a package, a safety device may be packaged separately from the unit proper and "forgotten" in an installation, or there may not be adequate protection against foreseeable mishandling en route. A large typewriter manufacturer, for example, showed a picture on one of its reports of the company's chief executive officer in front of a stack of cartons in a warehouse. The cartons were plainly marked "This side up" and "Do not stack more than five high." The stacks were ten-high, and over half the cartons were upside down.

Internal damage is a particular problem, as it may later cause injurious failure. Where internal damage is a possibility, checklists might incorporate the following concepts:

Safe, secure, protective packaging in line with the standards or custom of the trade or the state of the art.

Attachment or visible enclosure of all warning, installation, and use notices. It may be worthwhile to give each packer a photograph showing how these are to be tied to a unit or positioned next to it just before crating.

Incorporation, where appropriate, of shock and vibration devices to detect in-transit overstress.

Step-by-step packaging and crating procedures.

Written procedures for trucking, storage, and uncrating that are printed on the carton or readily accessible to all handlers from shipper to receiver.

Inspection. Inspection involves examining products and processes and detecting production deviations from the written specifications. In many firms this task is being expanded to include monitoring the specifications as well. But many firms depend too little on proper procedural safeguards in design and manufacturing and put the reject burden entirely on inspection. The "clinkers" that reach the customer are charged against a failure of inspection. The managerial error made here is that a function which carries an audit responsibility—inspection—is being corrupted into an extension of the production function. Our checklist calls for the following:

Check for accuracy of all specifications, manufacturing procedures, and standards.

Check for completeness of all specifications, manufacturing procedures, and standards.

Check for accuracy and completeness of all inspection requirements—in particular the performance of inspection procedures at the proper times along the production line.

Check for the actual performance of the inspection task. Make sure inspectors are not becoming more interested in production numbers than in quality standards.

Check for careful rework of rejects and "liability-conscious" methods of disposal of rejected items.

Check for completeness and accuracy of all production-run inspection reports, with proper sign-off procedures and records retention.

Warning. Finally, we come to the area of warning or labeling. After the *Miranda* decision, in which the U.S. Supreme Court ruled that a suspect must be advised of his right to keep silent and certain other rights, some police departments supplied their forces with small cards bearing the advice to be read to a suspect immediately following his arrest. That card, a form of checklist for the arresting officer, saved a lot of cases in court where the defendant claimed he had not been apprised of his rights. Similar reasoning holds true in product liability defense: The company must show that it apprised the customer of foreseeable dangers.

In many organizations, the responsibility for designing the content and format of instructions and warnings is diffused. Certainly the basic input must come from engineering and specification writers, but from here on the situation is not easily pinpointed. Let's look at two extremes. One firm's "instruction book" consisted of 1 page of installation instructions ("Call your local plumber") and over 35 pages describing the features of all other models in the product line. Another firm, producing a similar product, gave highly detailed instructions. For example, a certain visible input plug was mounted with a split collar and floating in a retainer. The instructions called attention even to this fact—namely, that this was a carefully designed safety feature and not a construction fault.

Our check items may be used by one department specifically charged with gathering information from design, engineering, and so forth and putting together all the written material a customer sees. Or the list may be broken into sublists for several departments. The checklist should cover such points as:

Label conformance to requirements of federal, state, and local regulatory agencies (e.g., FDA) regarding warnings in use.

Label conformance to industry standards, practices, and customs regarding warnings in use and (if necessary) dating.

Back-panel instructions for proper use and amplification of warnings.

Labels and use instructions that have the proper format, type size, language, comprehension level, and universal caution symbols.[14]

Carefully written and formulated user instructions for installation, use, and service that will be supplied with the product. The FTC is becoming particularly concerned with do-it-yourself products containing unclear instructions.[15]

A check that field-test feedback is incorporated in all of the above.

A check that the product's packaging for point of sale does

not in itself create unwarranted representations or foster carelessness in use.

This list is not exhaustive and is meant to supplement points developed throughout this book and items already present in company manuals. The list should be made specific to the operations of the firm and its particular products by a team of engineers, human-factors personnel, field service people, insurance loss-control representatives, the company risk manager, manual and label writers, test personnel, and systems-and-procedures-manual writers representing higher management interests.

Designing a checklist is an extremely difficult project. If it gets too long, it will not be used; if it is too short it affords no protection. The chief pilot of a large international airline, where use of a checklist is standard operation in the cockpit, expounded on his own philosophy regarding checklists: Use them where training or a manual cannot be made "goof-proof" for on-the-job use, but never as a substitute for training or a manual. Training gives the understanding that leads to intelligent use, and the manual is a thoroughly familiar, immediately accessible document for comprehensive and detailed backup.

The pilot recommends that checklists contain "do" statements only, that each statement be short but complete, and that statements be kept down in number to the bare minimum needed to do the job safely. As an example of reducing statements, he recalled a draft list that said: "Close A, close B, close C, upon landing." The three switches were, at his urging, provided with a "gang bar" to close them with one override motion, and the checklist now says "Close bar D upon landing." Similarly, a number of separate documents can be enclosed in one package; then a packing checklist need list only one step to assure their inclusion.

Items were added to or deleted from the airline list only after very careful deliberation and thorough proof that the action was proper. The crews were trained in the use of the checklist and required to use it at all appropriate times. Reliance on memory rather than physical use of the list—for a landing procedure, for example—resulted in heavy fines against the personnel involved.

Sales, marketing, advertising, and most other departments should have checklists of product liability prevention points. A newspaper article carried a story of a nine-year-old boy who was badly hurt when he attempted an "Evil Knievel Stunt Cycle" trick which had been demonstrated on TV.[16] Apparently the manufacturer, ad agency, and TV station never checked such considerations as the possibility of dangerous use, precautions against such use, and interpretation of the message by the young audience. Such cases offer ample support for the checklist concept.

External-relations documents

The third set of procedures which personnel should "work to" involves external relations. We include in this category a standby plan for public relations, a supplier's manual, and a customer relations manual.

Public relations procedures. Your firm's public relations representative is undoubtedly well used to "puffing" the firm's image under normal circumstances, but might be unprepared for a product catastrophe or recall situation. Consult with your attorneys and come up with a good, sensible modus operandi should you be hit with a publicized product-defect complaint or liability suit. Some attorneys will advise you to "button up" and say nothing, while others will have prepared elaborate public relations whitewash formats. Circumstances may not permit the luxury of the former, and experience has shown that a skeptical public reacts adversely to the latter, compounding the firm's difficulties. The position to adopt is individual to each firm and product, but it should be done in advance and not in panic. Above all, see to it that all personnel, under all circumstances, refrain from airing company problems which feed the plaintiff with free information.

Where you have problems that are of an industrywide nature or where the knowledge of other firms can be tapped on a mutual basis, have the trade association provide the vehicle for information transfer. If there are abuses of quality standards which smear all firms, again have the trade association work to correct the problems before government and regulations appear on the scene and plaintiff attorneys are provided with additional grist for their claims.

A specific procedure for the above should be adopted by top management and held as standby for the adverse product situation. It can then be implemented as standard operating procedure in dealing with the trade association.

Suppliers' manuals. Vendor-quality and vendor-relations manuals range from the sublime in complexity (those used in Department of Defense and NASA transactions) to very simple purchase-order forms. A supplier's manual should detail at least the following liability-prevention procedures:

Vendor quality and procedural checks to meet specifications.
Shipping-damage prevention.
Vendor insurance or special projects coverage.
Hold-harmless clauses in contracts.
Assumption-of-risk clauses.
Warranty details.
Prohibitions against substitutions without approval.

A small handbook printed by one firm, titled *Federal Government Documents for Quality Assurance,*[17] gives some indication of how complex just one aspect of procurement can be. The handbook identified 39 separate major documents governing quality and reliability procedures for armed forces and space contractors alone, and indicated that the list was only "a highlight of the more important items." Military quality requirements, inspection systems, calibration systems, electrical connections, and entire reliability programs were detailed, as well as a multitude of other requirements.

The points listed above are usually incorporated in contract policy manuals. Important aspects of contract law come into play here, requiring full review by the firm's counsel. Buyers should attempt to devise contract forms to meet specific conditions at specific plants and to word them to minimize possible liability responsibilities for actions and production outside their control.

Customer relations manuals. Customer relations manuals cover contract and field service activities. Later in this chapter we will document the roles of the departments involved, and the manuals needed will then become self-evident. For the meantime, we just suggest that the manuals cover at least:

> Contract review to eliminate any hold-harmless clauses, warranties, or unrealistic specifications which a customer might demand (e.g., purchase of a stripped or unsafe product to save money).
>
> Project engineering review of contract specifications to insure incorporation of safety features and prevention of the furnishing of mechanisms to short-circuit the features (which customers sometimes demand to increase production rates).
>
> Satisfaction of the purchasing agent's "best buy" requirements without unwise substitution of less safe materials or methods.
>
> Conformance to industry practices, codes, or standards with only very carefully approved deviations. Salesmen, negotiators, and engineers should be part of any team involved in setting standards for contracts, and exact procedures should be detailed in the manuals.
>
> Legal requirements, as drawn up by counsel, for the particular firm, product, and jurisdictions involved.

Audit Documents

We have given the label "audit documents" to the second category of documents because they relate to functions which neither create nor result in added value per se to the product. In an error-free, utopian world, performance by men and machines would meet the requirements of the previously discussed manuals and would self-monitor with checklists: we would need no audits.

We can best understand audits by examining their operation in the financial realm. Three levels of audit—which are separate and distinct from line operations—effectively standardize, provide methodology for, and monitor funds flow in the corporation. The board of directors will usually have a financial committee, the organization will have a controller's staff, and outside certification for operations will come from a certified public accountant. No one thinks of the controllership function as "costly" or as an invasion of the prerogatives of those who "have to put out and market a product," because it is traditional in business to watch the cashbox. And to operate without outside certification, whether or not it is publicly reported, is almost nonexistent in reputable firms.

When one looks at the product, however, few firms have anything resembling the three-tier type of monitoring outlined above. Under the old laissez-faire concept of mass production, the quality audit was aimed more at early defect detection to reduce rework costs than anything else. If marketing, engineering, and production people proved that a product would meet financial rate-of-return criteria, all other considerations fell by the wayside. The triangle of cost, quantity, and quality was definitely oriented to keep the latter at the minimum point the market would accept. Safety was a peripheral matter, of concern only to the corporate renegade—who received appropriate treatment in the firm's punishment-and-reward system.

The forces we have discussed throughout this book are bearing down on line management to add a product-oriented audit system comparable to that existing in the financial area. We suggest that this system also be a three-tiered one, with audits conducted by the board of directors, staff people, and external organizations.

Board-of-directors audits

Stockholder suits against members of boards of directors are becoming increasingly common, where, for example, financial mismanagement or insider stock manipulation is charged. It is becoming difficult and costly to buy directors' liability insurance, and fewer and fewer people are willing to serve on a board if their time is too limited to carefully monitor the details of financial statements. Stockholder suits generated by the repercussions of poor product quality are not beyond the realm of possibility. The day is not far off when a stockholder will sue because a product was not monitored, and the resulting catastrophic payouts will reduce dividends and damage the firm's credit rating, image, and trademark. Imagine the potential for lawsuits if a trademark worth millions in a goodwill accounting valuation were reduced to ashes by a catastrophe "the directors should have been alert enough to stop."

From all this, it is obvious that the first audit tier is the board of directors itself. The board should be provided with a short but complete manual of questions to ask about every existing product, model change, and new product. This document may be a simplified design-review checklist, a manual condensing all the other manuals discussed so far in this chapter, or a list of questions regarding what the company has done to prevent being charged with (1) strict liability in tort, (2) negligence in design, construction, test, inspection, or warning, (3) breach of express or implied warranty.

The choice of document is a matter to be discussed with house counsel and, perhaps, the insurance underwriter. The important point is that the questions be posed and the answers be supplied to the board or an appropriate subcommittee.

Staff audits

The second tier of audits is conducted by staff groups reporting to different levels of management. We are not aware of any trends toward establishing a single function for products comparable to the controllership, but some firms are moving toward or already have corporate quality control officers who can assume total direct and broken-line responsibility for corporate product safety.

The audits at this level as they presently exist come from the risk manager, from product safety engineers, and from quality control. As we discussed in Chapter 5, the risk manager identifies hazards, evaluates risk, and reduces or transfers that risk. Product safety engineers may be assigned to design, production, marketing, and other functions. They bring to bear an entire professional background in accident investigation and analysis, giving them strong credentials for auditing product safety and preparing and auditing the previously mentioned guideline documents.

Some firms group product safety engineers into a centralized safety department charged with some of the duties of the risk manager, such as development of:

Policies and decision guides for loss prevention.
Systems and procedures for execution of the policies, on a broken-line responsibility basis.
Loss and complaint information systems.
Auditing methods for new product safety.
Self-auditing procedures for all of the above.

The manual for this group would provide specifics for carrying out the above, including design review, communication procedures, measurement techniques, and specific product go/no-go approval powers. Without the latter, the manual will be attacked in court as a whitewash instrument rather than a serious and motivated hazard-elimination activity. Caution: Do not allow a situation to develop in which a no-go safety decision is reversed by management fiat. In addition to incurring exposure under strict liability or negligence, you may find that a business-risk exclusion in your policy leaves you with no insurance coverage.

The real brunt of internal audits should fall, we feel, on quality control. Later in this chapter we will discuss at length the expansion of the role of the quality control department, so we restrict our comments here to these facts:

1. Of all departments in a firm, this one has been most associated by the public with the responsibility for protecting the integrity of the product. Failure of a product is attributed by disgruntled users to "poor quality control" and not marketing (which fought for competitive pricing), production (which may have been careless or used substitute parts), or design (which is generally not understood by the layman juror).

2. Therefore, of all departments in a firm, the lack of a complete, comprehensive, and realistic (i.e., adhered to in practice) manual for this function will be most damaging in front of a jury.

3. Of all departments in the firm, this one has perhaps the furthest to go in rebuilding top management's respect for it. (See our comments on quality control in Chapter 1.)

We allude once more to the controllership function. Over the years it enhanced its position through practices and procedures developed by the accounting profession, which takes itself quite seriously both inside and outside the corporate context. Quality control personnel will have to emulate this model, and the place to start is better documentation of practices and procedures. Department of Defense standard MIL-Q-9858 expects its suppliers to demonstrate complete, self-policing, continuous quality controls appropriate to their product, people, processes, and facilities. It provides a good start for some company manuals. One author calls MIL standards "nothing more than well proven, usually very thorough, test requirements." He adds: "They represent excellent engineering and are used by the government buyer because they have, in most cases, stood the test of time and demonstrated their effectiveness." [18]

Other firms establish a dictionary of defects. These indicate how a product will look, function, and react to specific tests. Guides provide for differentiation between "major" and "minor" defects.[19] Auditing the product consists of matching its characteristics with dictionary guides and rejecting it for a major defect, or rejecting a batch for a series of minor defects.

External certification [20]

Finally, we come to the third tier of product audits: external certification. Here the corporation faces severe problems, many of which had their genesis in industrial obstruction of previous safety regulations.

Uniform standards for financial solvency were set following the crash of 1929. But no single event occurred early enough to give rise to uniform methods of certifying product safety. Today we have the following groups which all have to pass, separately in many cases, on the product:

Underwriters' Laboratories.
A use-test certifying laboratory.
An insurance loss-control group.
A federal test laboratory.
Consumer groups—whose informal "certification" may determine marketplace acceptance.

State regulatory agencies.

Local regulatory agencies (such as those of the City of Los Angeles, which require—among other things—certification of electrical and mechanical overload protection in consumer products).

Organizations that set standards for international trade.

Accreditation groups.

Certifications by these groups inevitably add a great deal of money to the cost of launching a new product, and they hurt the small firm the most. The increasingly severe dysfunctions created by these hurdles are most clearly seen in the case of a firm planning to introduce a new product or make major innovations in an older one. Sometimes the cost of innovation plus passing all the above tests (which have to be funded directly or through product modifications) will not be supported by marketing revenue—and the new idea is stillborn.

Following is a more detailed discussion of the nine groups listed above. To an increasing degree, a product will have to be certified by all or most of these groups before it reaches the ultimate market, and certain documents must be in-house.

Underwriters' Laboratories. This organization's testing procedures and standards are widely disseminated, and every engineer should have the appropriate documents at hand.

The fact that a component has Underwriter certification does not automatically make it fit for every conceivable use. Therefore, the design and testing teams in the manufacturer's plant should have for ready reference all documents pertaining not only to the finished product on which they are working, but also to each and every component they plan to buy or use from existing catalogues and for which a standard is available.

A use-test certifying laboratory. Gain experience in working with an independent test laboratory. It will, by virtue of its functional specialization, be able to come up with tests and specifications you may have overlooked. These documents should be on hand for ready reference.

Certification programs validated by an independent third party are covered by one of the standards developed by the American National Standards Institute. Standard Z34.1 makes clear that the certifiers must have no connection through management or financial stock arrangements with the product manufacturer or vendors of the product. But this, of course, does not preclude an exchange of information that will yield a better (safer) product.

An insurance loss-control group. Checklists used by insurance underwriters' loss-control groups are generally available to the interested insured party. Obtain and use these as references to prevent surprises when your products undergo an insurance audit and to pick up pointers for making the product safer.

A federal test laboratory. The Consumer Product Safety Commission maintains 14 field offices and product testing laboratories all over the United States. The National Bureau of Standards does testing, and various agencies such as the General Services Administration, the Department of Defense, and NASA, to name just a few, commission tests at government or private laboratories. The results and methodology are available for the price of reasonably diligent research and of the document itself. These federal records can provide enormous pools of information at very low total costs.

Consumer groups. A number of consumer groups test products and publish the results. In years past, even when a dangerous product feature was discovered, the manufacturer was unlikely to change anything if he deemed the risk small or the change costs high. Today, the results of these tests frequently are quoted in the media. It is unfortunate when such a testing service comes up with criticisms you should have designed out of the product on the drawing boards, but that is all the more reason to maintain an active file of test results on your own and competitors' products.

Services are also coming into being to advise, for example, purchasing agents of hospitals and physicians on the safety and efficacy of the instruments they buy. An instrument which receives a poor rating by one of these services, given the competition that is ready and willing to serve in its stead, is effectively knocked off the market. The reports and methodology of these services should also become reference material.

More and more services are bound to spring up to help the

purchaser who does not have the technical capability to evaluate the products he has to buy.

State regulatory agencies. While the drive for state certification of products has been blunted somewhat by the impact of the Consumer Product Safety Commission, it is important to note that letters of complaint do reach state attorneys general or consumer affairs commissioners. While their present efforts are geared mainly toward the licensing or certifying of service businesses and service technicians, it is only a short extension of their power to certification of products as well. The Consumer Product Safety Commission has held separate conferences with many state government representatives and hosted a huge conference of all 50 state representatives to mesh the powers of the states with those of the CPSC.[21]

Firms should, therefore, remain alert and collect documentation of (1) all state reactions and summaries of consumer complaints, and (2) all state actions with regard to certification of service-technician competency. Meeting the requirements for competency may act as a preventive against those product liability claims which arise from lack of care in installation or overlooking of detectable defects during the servicing of a product.

Local regulatory agencies. Local certification of products is now required before they can be sold in certain jurisdictions, or particular modifications must be incorporated for particular jurisdictions. As examples of possible problems, a local power company may deliver 208 volts to its customers' receptacles and only 220-volt appliances are sold there, or a customer may buy a 208-volt appliance and use it at 220 volts. While many appliances can take either combination, the fact that such a difference exists in what one might ordinarily believe is standard throughout the United States—namely, mains voltage—is indicative of the problems the manufacturer faces. His solution is to have his sales and field service personnel remain alert and send to the home office (1) all local codes and regulations impinging on product sale, use, and service; (2) all local product-certification test procedures; and (3) all local situational peculiarities which require forethought lest demands arise for more local certification. These documents should be duplicated and disbursed to all concerned.

Organizations that set standards for international trade. In 1970 the National Commission on Product Safety, in its final report, devoted an entire chapter to "Product Safety Abroad." It detailed consumer protection acts in Europe, Japan, and Canada with detailed tables of accidental death rates for 46 countries.[22] Three years later, at an engineering conference, a speaker asked a large audience how many had seen that material; a mere sprinkling of hands was the (rather frightening) response.

One major source of quality control information on an international scale is the United Nations Industrial Development Organization (UNIDO).[23] The American National Standards Institute (ANSI) interfaces with the International Organization for Standardization (ISO), the International Electrotechnical Commission, other international organizations, and various governmental commissions. ANSI's Committee Z1 is most concerned with this material. Its publications—and all other pertinent material—should be on the product manufacturer's shelves.

Accreditation groups. New standards for product performance are discussed almost daily by technical subcommittees of the medical, instrumentation, engineering, and other professional societies. Members of these subcommittees either serve on accreditation groups or directly influence them, so the standards they set for product acceptability are not to be taken as academic exercises. They may, for example, judge a medical instrument to be unsafe if under certain fault conditions it permits ground current above a certain level to flow through a patient. The professional organization may publish the standard, and the chief investigator on that committee may later be on a commission accrediting a hospital. Accreditation of a facility might be refused because, using the new standard as a guide, unsafe instruments are located there. If those instruments are of your manufacture, you will hear about the situation—if you had not already been kept informed. Aside from the accreditation problems, both you and the hospital have great liability exposure if the instruments remain in use.

The moral of all this remains very much with us: Keep current, and obtain the output of professional groups that publish suggested standards.

Conclusion

If we look back at the list of documents one should become familiar with just for an audit of his product, the lineup is indeed dismaying. It becomes doubly so when publications conflict in their safety suggestions or levels of acceptability.

Small increments in product safety can be enormously expensive, and one cannot lightly try to conform to the tightest specification without risking loss of a price-conscious market. We have no solution to the dilemma, but rest assured that the plaintiff attorney will find the tightest standard you violated and use it against you. If you know of the standard and you document your reasons for rejecting it, you and your attorney can try to explain your actions to the jury. If you were ignorant, your case is weakened accordingly.

Genealogy Tracing Documents

In the event of a product liability suit or a problem with the CPSC or OSHA, one of the first things you will have to do is collect all records pertinent to the individual product and to products made under the same conditions. It is here that the genealogy tracing system pays its way, by allowing you to pinpoint conditions as the product moved from design to market and to pinpoint the recall target if needed.

The life history of a product should be traceable from start to disposition by serial and model numbers or by batch and production-run numbers. (Production dating may also be helpful.) The ideal system of product traceability goes all the way down to serial numbers for each individual item, affixed in a permanent form. A suggested nameplate is shown in Figure 7 and discussed below. Consider using the most specific type of identification wherever possible and go to the broader ones only after due consideration. When a product liability lawsuit is a reality, demonstrating a sound traceability program may be vital to an adequate defense.

One large trade association was considering extending its tracing system into the customer's plant by affixing an embossed plate to each item that left its members' plants. A suggested

FIGURE 7. An embossed plate.

Owner/Operator

Stay up to date on this product. Send the following numbers:

Model XYZ123, Serial No. 1234567

and your

Name
Department
Company Address

to the following:

XYZ Company
Number and Street
City and State

XYZ will send you free job aids, literature, and safety information to help you do a better job in a safer manner.

plate was in the form shown in Figure 7. Members of this association were concerned not so much with first-sale customers but with resales, changes in customer-firm personnel, loss of caution notices, painting over of danger warnings, removal of safety features to achieve faster production, and so forth. While proof of these acts would relieve the product manufacturer of liability, the manufacturer still must prepare a legal defense against a suit and bear the costs of that defense.

The benefits of the nameplate will include the demonstration in court that you made an attempt to reach the operator with safety literature and proper operating instructions. In the case of second- and third-hand sales, if you receive letters instigated by the nameplate, your firm's contact people can visit the plant and, if safety features have been stripped, advise the owner accordingly. (A side benefit: Your marketing department has increased its potential customer list for new equipment.) The intent here is to place with the operator and owner of the product at least a share of the responsibility for keeping up to date in its use and remaining properly warned of the risks inherent in its operation. Thus the genealogy tracing system performs several duties at once and should be an essential part of a liability prevention effort.

We now take up the second major part of product liability prevention: program administration.

PROGRAM ADMINISTRATION

Program administration puts the document system to work. It is the organized, directed commitment of people and time to the use of the manuals and techniques available for making a liability prevention effort viable, continuous, and effective.

We will cover the administration of the program under five major topics. In the first, we briefly examine the role of top management and the role of the individual who may become responsible solely for liability prevention or (particularly in the small firm) may carry the responsibility along with several other major tasks. As our second topic, we bring up the relatively new concept of a design-review team; the product is given a total in-house review as it proceeds from concept to finished product by representatives of several departments working with a carefully designed series of questions. In the third section, we will examine the roles of various departments in preventing product liability. In our context we are dealing with a matrix organization, whereby each department will be expected to perform under the liability administrator while at the same time functioning in its routine line or staff capacity. In the fourth section we will discuss the sequential implementation of a liability-prevention program, geared to the three phases of a product's life cycle. And finally, in the fifth section, we will offer some brief tips to the liability defense team—should the firm become involved in litigation in spite of implementing all the concepts and reorganizations described in this book.

The Executive Role

Top management. The crucial step in product liability prevention is making top management aware of the problem and getting its commitment to establishing, maintaining, and enforcing product safety policies and procedures. OSHA and the changes in consumer protection laws have helped start the process. (And it has only started, as we discuss in the next chapter.)

The CPSC has the power to send company executives to jail. One major retail chain even designated a key senior vice president as "the one who goes to jail." [24] Following this, the vice president reportedly called his staff into his office and announced flatly: "There shall be no screwups." Such an attitude, when held by those with the real power and status in the organization, will result in effective, lasting liability-prevention efforts.

The liability-prevention administrator. The person who assumes responsibility for liability prevention may be the risk manager or the quality assurance director. The disadvantage of giving responsibility to the risk manager is that in large firms he may be so involved in the insurance aspects of the firm's business that he is unable to be sufficiently product-oriented to carry out the multifaceted aspects of the job. The alternative is to give responsibility to the quality control (or quality assurance) department. In some firms where this has been done, the department has assumed total control over vendor surveillance, design review, process studies, inspection of in-process goods, and analysis of field returns. Reaction to this has begun to set in. Harrington notes that at certain companies "[quality] engineers were expected to know more about human factors than the human factors engineer, more about the design than the design engineer, and more about the process than the process engineer." [25]

Such comments indicate the companies are making a mistake. The quality control function is properly an audit function; rather than performing the task, quality control should audit other people's work. To do this it would certainly not have to know "more about the process than the process engineer."

We believe a practical approach would be to blend the product safety director's position with a super-level quality control position and create a high-level "quality assurance director." Later in this chapter, under "Roles of the Various Departments," we will describe the expanded role of the quality assurance administrator at greater length.

Design Review

Boquist defines formal design review as "a scheduled systematic review and evaluation of the product design by personnel not directly associated with its development, but who, as a group, are knowledgeable in and have a responsibility for all elements of the product throughout its life cycle including design, manufacture, packaging, transportation, installation, use and maintenance, and final disposal." [26] Boquist calls it a management tool to help attain objectives—in our context, product liability prevention.

There is much controversy over when and how a design review should be performed. Some would review the product once when it is still a proposal, again during development of the design, and finally just after prototype. This is a decision each company has to make for itself, but we feel that if other precautions have been taken, repeated design reviews will not be necessary. In the first half of this chapter we detailed a series of guideline documents, checklists, and certification procedures. If such a documentation system is properly implemented, we assume that all persons connected with the product will follow to some reasonable extent the procedures contained therein. The procedures interlock in a check-and-balance fashion so that an error or omission by a group working to one manual would be picked up by a group working to a follow-on manual. And a new product already faces management, design, economic, risk, and market analyses in addition to those for safety.

Too early a design review, convening high-priced talent to discuss paper concepts, could turn into a fruitless bull session.

There must be something for the group to sink its teeth into. The real toss-up on timing is whether design review should be done after paper design is completed or after prototype-testing results are available. We suggest a combination approach: If prototypes are under the control of design and changes to the product are encouraged even after testing, a complete, formal design review can be conducted after prototype-testing. Prior to this, the firm could use subparts of a complete design review, such as failure-modes-and-effects analysis, fault-tree analysis, and human-factors analysis. These can be performed by the design and reliability engineers, and the results audited later by the full design-review team.

Failure-modes-and-effects analysis. This type of analysis considers catastrophic failure, partial failure, and wear-out of each component. The mode of failure (such as a switch jammed in the "on" position) and degree of user negligence (proper or improper use) are also considered. The effects of the failure are traced through the system, and the ultimate effect on the product's performance (and safety) is evaluated. One drawback of this method is that it considers only one failure type of one component at a time, and thus cumulative situations may be overlooked.

Fault-tree analysis. An undesired event is presumed to have taken place, and all possible occurrences that could have contributed to the event are diagrammed in the form of a tree. The branches of the tree are continued until independent events are reached. Probabilities are determined for the independent events, and after the tree is simplified, both the probability of the undesired event and the most likely chain of events leading up to it can be computed. This method requires a fairly heavy mathematical background in order for the user to obtain maximum benefits from it, although its use without extensive mathematical analysis is becoming more common.

Human-factors analysis. An analysis of the product in terms of its adaptability to the sensory, perceptual, mental, physical, and other attributes and capabilities of the human being using that product. In other words, human-factors analysis is the application of information about human behavior to the design of products and components. The primary concern in product liability prevention is with those factors which may have relevance to potential injury, involving anticipated use or misuse of a product by a human being. One method used for such an analysis is known as THERP—technique for human error prediction. Developed by the Sandia Corporation, it provides a means for quantitatively evaluating the contribution of human error to the degradation of product quality. THERP can be used for "human" components in a system and thus can be combined with either the failure-modes-and-effects or fault-tree method.

The function of the design-review team is to ask a series of detailed questions and obtain satisfactory answers. The team works from all the documents that can be assembled concerning the product's genealogy, all the standards and other documents that were used to guide its creation, and all test results available. Detailed design-review checklists are outside the scope of this book,[27] but it is not difficult to construct one simply from the considerations mentioned throughout this book and from good engineering principles. To give an example, questions may be asked on: use, foreseeable misuse, safety devices, packaging, shipping, warnings, labels, workmanship, human factors, failure modes, fail-safe provisions, noise/vibration/shock hazards, and reaction to temperature, overload, adverse atmospheres, sand, grit, or grounding. A full record of the entire analysis should be kept in writing, and every question posed must have an answer that will stand up when examined by a jury. If the product requires an assumption of risk by the user, for example, the design-review team should carefully note why this element of risk was left in the final product, and how the user was to be warned of his responsibilities for safety.

Roles of the Various Departments

In this section we discuss the roles of the different departments in reducing product liability exposure. Aside from top management, all department functions in relation to liability are broken-line or direct-line from the liability-prevention administrator to the line and staff groups. Thus a matrix structure exists. We have suggested that the administrator for liability prevention be the enhanced quality assurance director. This administrator, with the backing of management, should have authority inside the firm to divert resources to liability prevention and outside the firm to work with trade associations and consultants. At the risk of repeating ourselves, but for completeness of our presentation, we present highlights of the roles of major departments in the firm.

Quality assurance

The administrator may be responsible for all liability-prevention activities on a direct- as well as broken-line basis. The standard functions of this department are detailed in many excellent texts.[28] Its primary function is inspection of: incoming materials (both in-house and at vendors' plants), goods in process, and finished goods. It is important to note that the department should have *written* operating procedures, and these should accurately reflect actual operating procedures. As mentioned before, it is very damaging in court when testimony indicates that reality bears little relation to the book. The operating-procedures book must be kept current to the state of the art.

There must be standardized sets of quality control forms, performance statistics, and periodic progress reports showing inspections made and results found as a product moves down the assembly line. This product history record should be carefully retained in company files against the serial, production-run, or lot number of the product. The intent here is to show, in the event of a claim, that all possible care was taken during production to test every feature and item going into the product and to prevent products with bad features from being shipped to the customer.

Quality assurance should be able to supply standard operating procedures, copies of the forms used (kept up to date so that no "dead" forms exist), a description of all statistics kept, an accurate recording of yearly quality costs, progress reporting procedures, and records of all other practices of the department. These documents, if they accurately reflect what the firm actually does in the field of quality control, make a strong impression on judges and juries. It is important to note that one soft drink manufacturer has for years successfully defended itself against foreign-objects-in-a-bottle cases by demonstrating that its procedures are designed in such a way as to make this a virtual impossibility.

The functions of this department, in the enhanced form we recommend, include, first, overall administration of the design-review team. Quality assurance will determine who is tapped for the team, when it meets, what resources it needs, what procedures and forms will be used, and what results will be desired. Quality assurance will also defend the team against devitalization through absenteeism, withdrawal of support, or any of a host of organizational factors that can kill off a department whose function, in effect, is to inspect and comment on the affairs of other departments not directly subordinate to it on the organization chart.

Second, the department head will monitor the existence, maintenance, and support of the guideline documents, checklists, and external-relations material. While the actual writing of the manuals may be the responsibility of a systems-and-procedures group or the individual departments that use them, their existence, use, revision, and applicability should be audited by the quality department.

Third, this department head is to be informed of claims, of the results of claim analyses by risk management personnel, of returns from customers that are sent to engineering, of field service reports that indicate either premature failure or improper use, and of field audits of merchandise (buying or checking one's own product at the end of the distribution chain and giving it a thorough test and inspection). The latter is becoming an increasingly important function as companies find themselves responsible for the product even after its warranty has expired. Packaging is also being audited more carefully, through such devices as tiny shock indicators or sending recorders installed in dummy units which have the same packaging, and proceed through the same distribution chain, as the rest of the merchandise.[29]

In most firms, the data generated by multiple departments are never brought together in one format for complete analysis of all failures and correlation with materials, designs, etc., until a catastrophe occurs. The quality assurance department administrator should take the lead in seeing that this is done on a regular basis.

Finally, this department should have overall responsibility for the institution and maintenance of the genealogy tracing system.

Research and design [30]

This department inevitably knows more about the characteristics of the product and the materials of which it is composed than any other group. The main responsibilities of this group are to: (1) work from guideline manuals; (2) work to the state of the art; (3) be aware of courtroom-examination techniques and apply them to the product's design, potential construction, test, inspection, and warning; (4) provide inputs to the design-review team for its overall analysis or for subparts such as fault-tree analysis; (5) document decisions as to why certain safety precautions are not feasible and the risk is passed, with warning, to the user; and (6) maintain the widest possible acquaintance with all allied product fields so as to detect all possible hazards in use and misuse. In many design groups, reading is narrow and focused only on the product. A broad range of journals—including those on law, biology, medicine, and insurance—should be in the company library and their reading encouraged.

Product engineering

This department takes the paper design and should: (1) repeat the courtroom-examination techniques; (2) work to the guideline manuals; (3) check on materials selection and evaluation, particularly where reliability and fail-safe operation depend on the end use—e.g., on proper integration with customer equipment; (4) establish directions, cautions, warning notes, and labels for the user; (5) thoroughly test for the actual effects, on prototypes or pilot production items, of failure, marginal wear, and life exhaustion of the product and all its components—particularly the effects of cumulative failures; (6) establish the foreseeable limits of misuse and abuse; (7) perform a functional simplification in which unnecessary gadgets, parts, complications, or displays are eliminated; and (8) check that risk has been guarded against to the state of the art.

Manufacturing

This department has responsibility for the construction of the product. We feel this responsibility should include acting as a check against the decisions of the other departments by calling attention to such things as design features that cannot be dependably manufactured, by providing feedback to materials personnel when strength problems manifest themselves, and by being extremely careful about ordering production shortcuts or changes. Designers and engineers will specify tolerances and processes that may be extremely expensive. In some firms, manufacturing engineers will "improve" the specifications or change them to "an equivalent." The decision may then be ratified by a semi-disinterested designer or busy product engineer without full appreciation or evaluation of the effects of the "minor" change. The more prudent course for manufacturing to follow would be to apprise others of the specified process or tolerance and to elicit alternative specifications from design or product engineers. Manufacturing would then exercise semi-veto powers until a cost-effective solution was reached. In this way, the responsibility for the actual material or process would be clearly kept in design or product engineering with its attendant safeguards.

Manufacturing must insist on working to written procedures and must keep reality a direct reflection of those procedures. Perhaps the two biggest contributions that manufacturing can make to liability prevention are: (1) prevention of parts substitutions, process speed-ups, shortcuts, and other unsafe practices when the pressure is on for higher production; (2) detection and correction of process deviations. The latter includes backtracking to pick up and recheck every product that went through the line before, during, and after the time when deviations were most likely to have occurred.

Personnel

In an era when instant dismissal and a general inhumanity toward employees are not uncommon, this department must do everything possible to soften an employee's exit. As we discussed in an earlier chapter, today's ex-employee may be tomorrow's hostile witness.

On a more positive side, it is the responsibility of personnel to arrange for training in product safety and liability prevention. It may: (1) encourage attendance at conferences; (2) develop in-house courses and briefings; (3) inform all departments of university offerings; (4) support employee participation in standard setting by technical organizations. The latter is a particularly important activity on the international level, as indicated earlier.

In many firms, personnel is in charge of job specifications, position descriptions, and recording the hierarchical responsibilities of various departments. These should reflect the safety responsibilities and tasks detailed throughout this book.

Marketing

This department must be extremely careful not to create a situation in which breach of warranty may be charged, because in such cases consequential damages alone may run into enormous sums of money. Particularly when the firm is a supplier of capital equipment or industrial supplies, it is important that marketing not represent a product as safe under all conditions or put itself in the position of selling something that is patently not suited to the customer's requirements.

If a representative of the firm states that a product is safe under all conditions, this creates an express warranty that the product is indeed safe under all conditions, even though common sense tells us that somewhere some customer will subject it to conditions that make it unsafe. If an accident does take place, breach of the express warranty can be charged, and things can go badly for the defendant in court.

The other dangerous situation is when the customer relies on the seller to give him advice on which product he needs. If the salesman recommends a certain product or product feature and the customer relies on his advice, a situation of implied warranty is created: The seller has evaluated the situation and warranted that the item he is selling is fit for the use of the customer under the conditions in which the customer will store or use it. Too often, storage and operating conditions are overlooked. Again, if something goes wrong, a charge of breach of implied warranty can make a case go badly for the defendant.

Marketing personnel must be thoroughly familiar with the Consumer Product Safety Act, OSHA, and all related acts; with all certification standards in effect in all sales territories; and with product liability law. Salesmen, advertising people, and marketing analysts should be thoroughly briefed on the law and equipped with appropriate checklists.

Marketing personnel should be "the eyes and ears" out in the field. They should detect misuse and abuse, watch for situations where safety features and protection seem needed, evaluate whether existing equipment needs state-of-the-art safety upgrading, and note the competition's equipment and features. Marketing should also have a carefully delineated procedure to follow if a salesman detects a possible liability situation, a threat of a claim, or a simple complaint that may easily turn into a claim. This procedure, as we mentioned in Chapter 5, must be drawn up by counsel and the insurance underwriter.

Marketing people should take part in contract review, in which they and counsel review all agreements to guard against undesirable hold-harmless and warranty clauses. The risk manager will also work with marketing, to review contracts that represent undue exposure to liability claims because the buyer specifies unsafe products to cut his costs or does not have proper storage facilities for what he purchases. The risk manager will also look out for situations where sales people enter into contracts for operations and services not covered by the firm's insurance policy. Marketing should clear unusual contracts with the risk manager before signing them, lest the firm be committed to an uncovered liability situation.

Finally, marketing should review all advertising to insure that the audience appreciates that while the product has been made as safe as possible, there is risk in using anything and certain precautions should be observed. This is particularly important when the audience is children.

Purchasing

The traditional role of this department is to obtain supplies that meet the specifications set up by those with authority to order. Purchasing seeks to provide proper quality, proper quantity, and timely delivery at the lowest possible cost.

This role must be enlarged to include liability prevention through: (1) carefully framed contracts with vendors (worked out with counsel) to clear up liability responsibility before any problems arise; (2) a push for quality-certification programs in vendor plants; (3) alertness to new safety features and components marketed by vendors and circulation of this information for use by research and design, product engineering, and other departments.

Field engineering and maintenance

This department plays a key role when the firm's customers are industrial or commercial users of supplies or equipment. We think this department should include highly trained (technically, legally, and psychologically) accident investigators. Upon receipt of a notice, complaint, threat of a claim, or claim, this group will be charged with gathering all the evidence at the scene of the injury and all attendant environmental information. This department should work closely with design, product engineering, and quality control to trace the genealogy of a product failure and help prepare the legal defense if product misuse and abuse are evident.

On a broader scale, field service can report on general environmental conditions encountered in customer plants; pay irregularly scheduled visits (if possible) to see equipment in operation; inspect all safety features, using a checklist; and warn customers in writing when safety devices have been bypassed.

This department is also charged with sending out hazard notices, recommending repairs, and performing them directly or through contractors when failures show that a design or construction feature is unsafe. The department will help with on-the-job instruction, replace missing caution notices, and bring products up to the state of the art if the customer so desires and is willing to pay a reasonable cost. This latter point is a good way to build a defense against a future claim that a product is unsafe. The customer is notified that advances in the state of the art can be incorporated in his device for a reasonable service fee. Should he turn down this service, he can be held to have had due notice and opportunity to render the product safe, but refused to do so—and he shoulders the liability.

Field service engineers will often request that instructions and precautions for products be printed in more than one language. While this approach is quite common in Europe, it is not yet the rule in the United States, in spite of the courts' stringent definition of what constitutes adequacy of warning (see Chapter 2). When a user cannot read a warning or instruction, the engineer or maintenance person on the scene will usually instruct him in his language, but this is makeshift and not much of a courtroom defense.

In a large firm, field service will often be looked upon as a loss leader and cut accordingly in times of financial stress. However, a more healthy attitude is to view it as feedback from the customer on how the product is actually performing in the field and on precisely what happens when its performance deviates from standard. Field service should provide information to research and design, product engineering, and other departments working on hazard analysis, and its contribution should be valued accordingly.

We have covered the operations of those departments we feel play key roles in liability prevention. But the ones we left out by no means stand aloof from the problem. The management commitment to safe products should effectively key all concerned departments into the loss-control effort, through the matrix organizational structure which ties them to quality assurance.

Sequential Implementation

Our next area of interest concerns the three major parts of the product life cycle: pre-customer, in customer use, and post-customer.

Pre-customer phase

Throughout this chapter we have covered the major company activities pertinent to the product from its inception to shipping. Here we will add to this discussion by touching briefly on the rest of the distribution chain.

The wholesaler and retailer will be joined (made codefendants) in any product liability suit. While the exact nature of their liability under warranty law will be open to question in each case, negligence on their part will almost surely put them in a poor defense position.

The wholesaler's liability exposure increases with the number of acts he performs on the product. At one extreme he may simply be a broker who buys and sells on the telephone, never even seeing the product. He may provide warehousing services and nothing more if he acts as a true wholesaler. At the other extreme he may buy in bulk and repackage for retail sale. In the case of the broker, it would be difficult to show breach of warranty or negligence unless he performed some marketing role and created a warranty expressly or by implication. The warehousing type of wholesaler may be open to negligence-in-handling charges (e.g., having created hidden damage by rough handling, leading to premature or disastrous failures). The repackaging type of wholesaler is wide open to breach-of-warranty and negligence charges. Incidentally, it is not unusual for economically marginal wholesalers or distributors to skimp on labeling, use instructions, or even proper packaging. They have taken on a manufacturer's responsibilities without his resources in money, manpower, or talent—and sometimes without even the desire to protect themselves properly against product liability claims.

Regardless of the degree of participation of the wholesaler, however, we must offer one major precaution to the manufacturer: The distributor or wholesaler is part of the genealogy tracing system, and he must be urged to keep careful shipping records so that products can be tracked down by serial number or production run. The intelligent, prudent manufacturer will periodically audit the record keeping of its distributors.

The retailer is also open to warranty and negligence

charges. Through its salespeople, the store recommends products for different uses, and often these salespeople know less about the product than the customers. Many products—bicycles, toys, furniture, outdoor gear, and so forth—come as collections of parts. The store which services its customers by assembling these items must do so with all due care lest it be charged with negligence in construction. Salespeople should be instructed to turn over to the customer all instruction booklets, warning labels, and other cautionary notices that came with the product, lest the store be charged with negligence in warning of risks. A checklist system for salespeople would find good application here.

As liability insurance coverage becomes increasingly costly, it is not unreasonable to expect that manufacturers will try to limit their losses by shifting responsibility down the distribution channel when a product-related injury or damage occurs. Wholesalers and retailers can try to defend themselves by doing only the bare minimum to the product at points of distribution and sale, and by exercising great care with checklisted procedures in handling the product.

In-customer-use phase

The second phase of interest to us is the time during which products are in use by the customer. More and more companies are using employees as product testers to obtain feedback on pilot production, are using carefully tracked test marketing to detect premature failures and unforeseen uses (in addition to evaluating sales potential), and are making intensive warranty analyses. Since the first two practices are self-explanatory, let us focus on the third one for a moment.

There are two types of warranties used: [31] (1) that in which the consumer returns a card and "registers" his product; (2) that in which a long explanation of what the manufacturer will do for the consumer is part of the instruction or installation manual and the consumer need do nothing.

The former type requires some discussion. The registration warranties for some products can be quite complex, as is the case for certain cameras. Sending in the card yields return of a date-punched, signed warranty that makes available extensive, worldwide free services for a year or more. Other registration cards look more like market surveys, and consumers dispose of them without a thought. If your cards are of this type, it is prudent to reshape their content and convince the consumer he is helping himself by returning them. Warranty registration is part of your genealogy tracing system.* Also, where big-ticket items or complex items are sold, retailers should be encouraged to enter names, addresses, and product model numbers in a clear fashion on the sales slip.

Products returned for repair under warranty should be extensively and intensively analyzed. Mundel [32] cites a number of techniques for analyzing warranty and field service failure data. He suggests Pareto analysis for failure causes (to highlight the important ones first), analysis of parts replacement trends, and military failure-analysis systems such as FARADA (failure rate data). The latter focuses on parts failure, stress, and environmental data from which reliability forecasts can be made. Mundel's recommendations include: specific assignment of the data-gathering responsibility; maintaining records of calls, repairs, and environmental conditions; extending the change-control system into the field as well as the plant; and establishing channels for emergency evaluation of unusual incidents. Mundel takes a cost-benefit approach to the subject—i.e., studies of field warranties and their follow-on service can yield information that will reduce costs in future designs of production—but his ideas obviously apply to liability prevention as well.

Post-customer phase

The post-customer phase involves product recall, analysis, and disposal. We have already discussed the insurance aspects of recall, and product analysis is obviously a technical job done by engineering people, so we will limit our present discussion to disposal.

---

* Incidentally, you might want to tell the consumer that his sales slip or canceled check will be used to date the warranty, to cut down on those consumers who try to fudge on dates by sending in the card only after a fault is detected.

The prime example of a product-disposal disaster is the too frequently reported case of the child who is suffocated in a discarded refrigerator. Many municipalities now have ordinances requiring removal of the door before disposal, and manufacturers have also solved the problem with the magnetic latch. However, visualize the liability exposure should one manufacturer have let his door operation lag behind the state of the art.

Batteries, aerosol cans, and many other products carry caution notices in regard to their disposal. Again, the prudent manufacturer will consider what could happen to his product when its exhaust life has been reached—or before. Before it is completely worn out the product may go into a used market or, as is true of many government items, to schools or prisoner-training programs. There, less sophisticated users will be exposed to it, and the item is far removed from the environment that the design-review team once had in mind.

Finally, we once again call attention to the matter of packaging. Disposal of packaging material is becoming a serious problem—as, for example, in the case of the highly flammable container that caused incinerator explosions in apartment houses. While most of the resultant fires were contained and yielded no litigation, the public concern with environmental pollution will surely result in product liability suits for recovery of society's cost in handling packing-waste and product disposal (such as a built-in, customer-paid fee for auto disposal at the time a new car is purchased).[33] The hundreds of proposed measures to ban or regulate various forms of packaging could reduce large investments in machinery to little value virtually overnight. While packaging has helped increase retail productivity by making self-service possible, careful consideration of its dysfunctions is necessary to avoid future liability exposure.

The Defense Team

Despite use of all the foregoing documents, procedures, and checklists, it is still true that the clinker will get through and there will be injury or damage. The time to prepare for difficulties is before one is hit with a claim, not on an ad hoc basis for each event.

We laid the groundwork for defense by emphasizing genealogy tracing, which facilitates pulling all the records pertinent to a product; field service, which moves to investigate the incident on site; and the role of the attorney who heads the defense team. The latter team is our focus here.

In Chapter 2 we extensively analyzed the role of the plaintiff attorney's engineer. His counterpart on the defense side is the number one assistant to the defense attorney. Insurance representatives, quality control personnel, and members of the design-review group should be detailed to aid the attorney and his engineer whenever necessary and should become familiar with one another even before becoming involved in litigation. If an outside consultant is retained, he should be made as familiar with the firm and the product as its own personnel.

The defense attorney acts as adviser to management, may help personnel conduct its briefings on product liability prevention, and should periodically sweep internal files of certain types of potentially damaging material. The latter is one of the most important areas in which the defense team can function before litigation. Defense attorney Warren Eginton calls in-house memoranda the most dangerous type of record.[34] They are often written in draft with conflicting positions noted, and may even, we have found, show damaging non-resolution or "political" resolution of problems, or awareness of problems and then virtual disregard of safety to reduce costs. Eginton bluntly states that in-house memoranda (particularly those containing statements of position) and drafts of letters should not be kept. In one firm, for example, in-house attorneys visit plants around the country at least once a year to sweep the files of material which the opposition in potential litigation could use in a damaging way. At each plant, the defense team meets with the attorneys for one or two days and all files are examined closely.

The defense team should be reasonably well trained in relevant areas of the law—from contracts to negligence—and should have actual courtroom exposure, testimony experience (even practice sessions help), and general exposure to product liability cases through readings of various case-reporting publications.

IN SUM

This chapter has focused on loss prevention as an activity which must exist throughout the organization. If not already part of the perceived roles of executives, engineers, salesmen, and the like, loss-prevention activity should augment their present activities and become thoroughly integrated with them.

We hope the reader has not become discouraged by the sheer quantity of actions and procedures that have been suggested. In attempting to cover all facets of liability prevention, we may, in true bureaucratic fashion, have gone overboard in places. However, we would like to point out that the program can be grafted onto most existing operations and basically requires only a change in orientation—to include safety as a prime parameter in product decisions—for reasonable success. It must be remembered that the product and the firm will be judged by a jury of reasonable people. If they see that the firm took all due care—with the documents and procedures we have described—it will be very difficult for plaintiff attorneys to penetrate "the deep pocket." And the product will indeed be a safer one.

REFERENCES

1. *Final Report of the National Commission on Product Safety* (Washington, D.C.: U.S. Government Printing Office, 1970).
2. William V. White, "The Consumer Product Safety Act and Its Administration," *Chemical Technology* (May 1974), p. 286. Reprinted with the permission of the American Chemical Society.
3. Ibid.
4. "Dictating Product Safety," *Business Week* (May 18, 1974), p. 59.
5. White, op. cit., p. 287.

6. Public Law 91-596, 91st Congress S.2193, December 29, 1970.

7. *Federal Register, 1972*, Department of Labor, Occupational Safety and Health Administration, Vol. 37, Nos. 202, 203, and 243.

8. "Be Prepared," *Trial*, Vol. 9, No. 4 (July–August 1973), p. 15.

9. See Steuart Henderson Britt, *Consumer Behavior in Theory and Action* (New York: John Wiley & Sons, 1970), pp. 266–267.

10. Harry M. Philo, "Use of Safety Standards, Codes and Practices in Tort Litigation," *Notre Dame Lawyer*, Vol. 41, No. 1 (November 1965), p. 2.

11. Ibid., p. 7.

12. "Paris Crash Laid to Faulty Door," *The New York Times*, April 9, 1974, p. 25.

13. Dwight J. McDonald, "Keeping Track of Design Modifications," *Machine Design* (February 21, 1974), pp. 92–96.

14. See *Recommended Precautionary Labels* (Washington, D.C.: National Paint, Varnish and Lacquer Association, 1967) for a number of recommendations.

15. "Do-It-Yourself Items to Be Tested by F.T.C.," *The New York Times*, August 7, 1973, p. 22.

16. "Father Sues for 24 Million," *Long Island Press*, May 9, 1974, p. 1.

17. Product Assurance Council, General Precision Systems, Inc., 1967.

18. P. J. Riley, "How to Choose an Independent Testing Laboratory," *Machine Design* (March 7, 1974), p. 88.

19. "What Customers Call Quality," *Quality Progress* (March–April 1973), pp. 12–13. See also the U.S. Department of Defense's Military Standard MIL-STD-105D, from which many dictionary meanings may be derived.

20. For an excellent review of the liability of certifiers of products and the protection which a manufacturer gains through certification, see "Liability of Certifiers of Products for Personal Injuries to the User or Consumer," *Cornell Law Review*, Vol. 56, No. 1 (November 1970), pp. 132–147.

21. "Dictating Product Safety," op. cit. The conference was held on the first anniversary of the CPSC.

22. *Final Report of the National Commission on Product Safety*, op. cit., Chapter 11.

23. See UNIDO's "Guides to Information Sources," particularly *Information Sources on Industrial Quality Control*. Available from

Industrial Documentation Unit, UNIDO, P.O. Box 707, A1011 Vienna, Austria.

24. "Dictating Product Safety," op. cit., p. 59.

25. H. J. Harrington, "The Last Step from QC to QA," *Quality Progress* (May 1974).

26. Edwin R. Boquist, "Tutorial on Formal Design Reviews," *Proceedings, Product Liability Prevention Conference, 1973* (Newark, N.J.: Newark College of Engineering, 1973), p. 75. See also Kurt Green et al., *Failure Mode Effects and Criticality (FME and CA) Analysis Procedure for Equipment Safety Assessment*, Document PB194188 (Springfield, Va.: National Technical Information Service, U.S. Department of Commerce, 1970).

27. See Boquist, op. cit., pp. 77–80. Write to PLP Conference, Newark College of Engineering, 323 High Street, Newark, New Jersey 07102 for a copy of the *Proceedings*.

28. Joseph M. Juran's *Quality Control Handbook*, 3rd ed. (New York: McGraw-Hill, 1974) is perhaps the bible of the professional.

29. "Quality Assurance Enroute," *Quality Management and Engineering* (April 1974), pp. 24–26.

30. See Frank C. Jose, Jr., *R&D's Role in Product Liability* (New York: AMA, 1970).

31. Jon E. King, "The Written Product Warranty," *Quality Progress* (January 1973), pp. 28–33.

32. August B. Mundel, "Product Evaluation via Warranty Analysis," *Proceedings, Product Liability Prevention Convention, 1971* (Newark, N.J.: Newark College of Engineering, 1971), pp. 143–152.

33. Tom Alexander, "The Packaging Problem Is a Can of Worms," *Fortune* (June 1972), pp. 105–107, 194–202.

34. Warren W. Eginton, "Minimizing Product Liability Exposure," *Quality Progress* (January 1973), pp. 22–23.

7

CLOSING
THOUGHTS
Avoiding Problems in the Future

In this chapter we take a somewhat more future-oriented approach to liability prevention. To a large degree, this will involve buttressing and summarizing many of the major points we have been making throughout the book. We will not, however, repeat our warnings about inadequate insurance coverage. We believe we hammered on the point sufficiently in Chapter 5: Take great care in analyzing and reviewing your insurance policies.

We suggest five ways in which the manager can guard against future liability problems—many of which are unforeseeable. First, we urge that you follow an obvious path: improve the product. Second, we suggest exerting pressure on your company and trade association to better educate the consumer. If the consumer knows that your product is safer, your sales will not be undercut by a marginal competitor who offers a lower-priced but less safe product. Third, we once more emphasize the need to be continuously prepared for liability litigation. Fourth, we offer some thoughts on the need for management to place more emphasis on quality and safety. And finally, we suggest that you be continuously alert to changing conditions—the climate of consumerism, the evolution of the law, and the potential impact of these factors on your firm.

IMPROVE THE PRODUCT

Legal action will generally not be sustained against you unless your product is "unreasonably dangerous" or "legally defective." Remember that the definitions of these terms vary in different courts and at different times. "Unreasonably dangerous," as we noted in Chapter 1, means dangerous to an extent beyond that contemplated by the ordinary consumer with ordinary knowledge—but the interpretation of this varies. Generally your product will be judged "legally defective" if the following conditions exist: [1]

1. Your product carries a significant risk to consumers and they do not anticipate or guard against such risk.
2. The degree of risk is sufficiently great that foreseeable use poses a danger to the user. (In some cases even misuse of the product is included.)
3. You, as a seller, did not work at the state of the art or did not know about the risks even as you marketed the product and generated a use for it.

You should reduce as many risks as possible and warn the user against the remainder. Hindsight in the midst of litigation puts the firm in a bad light. We do not always know that our products carry a significant risk and are unreasonably dangerous, but sometimes we should be able to infer from common knowledge and good sense that our processes yield a potentially dangerous product.

Major U.S. firms were among those caught in the "great tea-kettle scandal," in which Canadians learned their national drink was poisoning them. A nurse traced high lead levels in a baby's blood to a tea kettle and triggered a massive government investigation. Lead was being released in dangerous amounts into the boiling water from the solder used in making the kettles.[2] As soon as the Canadian government finishes testing all suspect models of kettles, it plans to review all products used in the storage, preparation, and serving of food.[3]

Should the firms have known that lead could be released by their products? We answer by pointing out that the Food and Drug Administration has, during the past ten to fifteen years, been repeatedly trumpeting the dangers of certain lead ceramic salad bowls imported from abroad. Why, then, did sophisticated firms with the ability to learn and test not discover and prevent the lead problem in their own products? A cynic in the industry, off the record, says "they didn't want to look"—and calls attention to the fact that silver solder is very much more expensive than lead.

In medicine today, we are using stronger drugs and new techniques and devices. There are certain to be long-term consequences of which we are not aware, just as the innovations in medicine made shortly after World War II have begun to have unfortunate side effects now.[4] We say in hindsight that the manufacturers should have known, should have reduced the risks, and should not have inflicted them on unknowing or inadequately protected consumers.

The most drastic action that you as a manager can take is to produce no product, or merely to market the products of others with strong hold-harmless agreements protecting you so that the other party bears the brunt of a suit. On a more practical level, however, we suggest that you check the state of knowledge when your people first conceive of a product to fill a market gap or consumer need. If your product is being tailored to a specific use for a specific customer, be doubly vigilant. What is the customer going to do with the product? Will it do the specialized job you are tailoring it for? What kind of abuse and misuse might he give it? If you can't guard the end user against his own folly, and he can't be adequately taught to use the product, and he "refuses" to be warned about misuse or satisfied with contemplated performance, perhaps the product idea is best discarded. You may guard yourself against some problems by strictly defining contract terms, but in injury cases the courts brush these aside fairly readily.

When you get into the design phase you must ask yourself

if all the hazards are truly known. Are you leaving yourself open to a "tea-kettle scandal" by not specifying the safest materials or processes? What tradeoffs are you making, if any? If a particular hazard is well known in allied products (other products that come in contact with food, for example), do you apply the knowledge to your own product as well?

Knowledge of hazards is becoming more and more available every day. The National Highway Traffic Safety Administration, for example, is appealing to the public for information on timing gear failures.[5] If this approach is successful in generating useful first-hand information, it will surely be used by other agencies as well. The Food and Drug Administration inherited the start of a National Electronic Injury Surveillance System [6] from the National Commission on Product Safety, and the system will probably be expanded nationwide. It yields, by a touchtone telephone system directly wired into a computer, data on product-related injuries that come to the attention of hospital emergency rooms. The system started with 14 hospitals in two areas and by 1974 had been expanded to 119 hospital emergency rooms in 30 states.[7] The National Commission on Product Safety also carried out a comprehensive survey of product liability insurance, a survey of physicians, and a death-certificate analysis

Other organizations, such as insurance companies, have information that is germane to existing or contemplated products. If they don't, get your trade association to do the job. Make sure that your designers and engineers broaden the range of journals they read, the breadth of the conventions they attend, and the scope of their activities in professional associations. Whenever possible, key into the experiences of other firms through these contacts, so as to avoid relearning expensive lessons.

When the product moves into prototype and pilot production, make sure you have a real, down-to-earth design review and some thorough use tests. The outside test lab that tells you a product is unsafe (after all the procedures you have followed to make it safe) probably has saved you a high multiple of its fee—assuming its criticisms are well grounded. If you change the design and then pass their certification tests, this is impressive evidence that you tried to make your product as safe as possible. A reputable test laboratory will not knowingly certify an unsafe product, because if it does—and the plaintiff's attorney can prove that it did—the liability damages may be assessed against the laboratory in any ensuing litigation.

In constructing the product, adopt the attitude "there shall be no screw-ups"—not only because you don't want to run afoul of the law, but because you want to put out a product that your personnel will not point to with disdain. Your vendors should not be able to use your company's operations as examples of the lowest common denominator. Impress upon them that if they run out of material X they cannot substitute material Y until the latter is checked out by a design-review team.

One firm had to repair defective valves on 15,000 built-in gas ovens.[8] The vendor of the valves had substituted ½-inch pipe after running out of the specified 1-inch pipe. This created complications in later assembly of the valves to the stoves, and gas leaks developed. To add insult to injury, CPSC engineers later found 11 other defects in the same valve. Why did the vendor switch from specifications and then turn out sloppy products? Because he knew in advance that he was dealing with a firm which so disregarded its responsibilities to test and inspect that it would probably allow defective components to be assembled on thousands of its own products. He knew in advance that he could shave pennies per valve by cutting design and inspection in his plant. After all, so did his customer.

You want to put out a product that is known by "the quality it keeps." Some time ago, the industry leader for one consumer electronic product switched from wired to printed circuits. It had difficulties with its sets that should never have reached the sales floor, let alone a consumer. When troubles developed, the competition began trumpeting its "hand-wired" sets and took away the market lead. The average consumer hasn't the faintest idea what a circuit board is, but these consumers had heard from friends, from repairmen confronted with serious problems, and from other mysterious sources that "wired sets are better." Their purchase decisions were affected accordingly.

Audit what goes on in your plant and the product which reaches the ultimate user with the care you devote to auditing cash flow. Make sure your people have precise functions, have well-designed checklists to help them perform them, and are backed up by up-to-date manuals. If you can't make up your own checklists, seek help from insurance underwriters, consultants, your trade association, or professional organizations. The National Safety Council, for example, has been publishing self-evaluation checklists to help firms rate their own preparedness in meeting OSHA requirements.[9] The same is being done for product liability avoidance, by the diverse groups mentioned above.

If you are designing, building, or packaging to any "official" or "industry" standards, try to make sure they are not an industry-oriented, lowest-common-denominator whitewash of existing practices. If they are, beat them with your own standards—and make internal compliance with these standards mandatory.

Sampling plans cause a great deal of difficulty, and the standards for acceptance or rejection must be as tight as possible. If a bad product gets through, you will suffer through strict liability in tort. To mitigate your damages you will have to show that you tried to weed out defective products. Some people suggest the introduction of a system of "legally acceptable sampling," in which the lot size is made very small. Finding one defect in the sample would require 100 percent inspection of the lot, 100 percent inspection of the production run, or some smaller percentage of inspection. This decision can only be made by each manufacturer. He knows whether the only definitive test available will also destroy the product, and how much damage a product failure will probably cause versus what the cost of inspection would be in manpower, equipment, and slowing the production lines.

New methods of inspection should not be overlooked. There may be a new, nondestructive method or an automated method that allows 100 percent inspection and is fast, economical, and definitive. Your sampling plan will be destroyed in court if the state of the art would have allowed the applications of such a system to your product at the time it was built.

When the product reaches the ultimate user, don't lose track of him. Tell the consumer why he should return the warranty registration card, instead of confining its apparent function to asking him whether he bought the product or received it as a gift. Getting consumers to send in cards should be a trade association public-education mission, coupled with a content "reform" on the part of each manufacturer.

Whether you "outboard" the warranty (give the dealer a discount on his product cost as insurance against future service costs) or "inboard" the warranty service (dealer pays full price but bills the manufacturer for service under warranty), audit your system to make sure all complaints are documented thoroughly and reach your quality control and design people for failure-trend analysis. If repair services are performed by a company division, so much the better for controlling documentation. Whenever the documents are not completely filled in down to the last part number, or whenever failed parts are not returned to you, charge the dealer or your division accordingly and do everything you can to force compliance. Those failure reports are important.

You should also maintain the flow of documents on post-warranty repairs. You may have to pay the service organization to fill in and send you the forms, or you could send your quality control personnel into repair shops for random sampling of service problems. Above all, do not, as one retail chain did, classify safety problems under "miscellaneous" when presenting consumer complaints to top management for analysis.[10] Remember that early attention given to a complaint or threat may prevent it from turning into a liability, and a suggested rule of thumb is that one complaint represents the problems of at least 1,000 customers.[11]

The courts have held that it is the duty of the manufacturer to improve his product—to make it safer as the state of the art advances. This means that even a best-selling, high-volume item cannot be kept static in design if improvements that guard against or reduce user risk become possible. To improve a product, therefore, means not only adding competitive features or reducing its costs or increasing its performance capability, but a very real effort to increase its safety.

EDUCATE THE CONSUMER

If the product has been made safer, educate the consumer to want safety in spite of what appear to be insuperable obstacles to doing so. Sales departments strenuously resist selling safety because of its negative connotations. Some corporation officials stress the fact that the bulk of the circulation of consumer journals is in the Northeast, and that even the leading publication has a circulation that is only a fraction of some popular sex magazines. Too many managers point to the experience of the Ford Motor Company when it tried a safety-oriented campaign with its new padded dashboards and safety belts in the mid-1950s. A surface impression of the sales data showed that the company lost ground to its competitors—and the safety advertising campaign was faulted. More recent analyses have led to unofficial but nevertheless convincing conclusions that Ford's sales losses would have been far worse *without* the safety focus.

Physics, chemistry, and biology have been eliminated from core course requirements in most college liberal arts programs, and their strength in high school leaves much to be desired. Vocational arts have been downgraded as students are exposed to more "educational" or "cultural" pursuits. Thus, the average person has little or no technical background on which to base his product purchase and use decisions.

Overcoming the education gap between what the consumer knows and what he should know has four phases:

1. Start by making every effort to educate the children in schools. Companies spend hundreds of thousands of dollars per year on films they distribute free. These films are reviewed by teachers and college instructors for possible use. Most are so bad—flagrantly distorted, self-puffing, facile commercials geared

to the mentally retarded—that it is virtually impossible to sit through an entire screening. If your company is serious about safety, divert some of this public relations money into imaginative educational material. Get your trade association to do the same. Take into account that the recipient's knowledge of physics, chemistry, and biology is close to zero. View this not as a hurdle but as an opportunity to educate the recipient and give him a working knowledge of the pertinent subject. You want him to be able to judge the desirability of your ground fault interrupter for his pool, to know that your unit is equipped with better guards or is better constructed, to know how to more safely use what he buys from you. The more educated he is, the less likelihood of injury or damage. And in the event of a lawsuit, such education can help support a claim by your attorney that the consumer knowingly assumed certain risks in using your product or, by not following instructions, abused and misused the product. Someday a defense attorney will be able to introduce to the jury a booklet, film, or other medium on "how to safely use products like X." Defense counsel will establish that the medium was used in the injured party's schoolroom—that he saw it and knew about its warnings, risks, and performance requirements—yet he failed to heed the material and contributed to or even caused his injury.

Schools should also get across the message that reading the instructions is a must before operating any piece of equipment or even playing with a toy.

2. Next, review your advertising. Don't claim more than your product can do; rather, aim at least part of your appeal to the most rational, well-informed consumer you can imagine. Often this consumer will be a professional in the field. We recall the marketing philosophy employed by a once-small camera importer. He loaned equipment—often for long, indefinite periods —to professionals in the photography field. He used feedback from them to make the supplier upgrade his already superior product, enhancing its features and operation. The professionals soon spread the word, and other professionals began buying. The importer then advertised the camera as "the choice of the professionals." He did not have to "buy" their endorsements

beyond the initial loans because his product was everything he said it was.

In the same vein, if you really have a safe product, and a good one, make the satisfied user your best salesperson. There are enough testing organizations that will provide a legitimate safety certification which you can advertise. Here you are educating the consumer using the testing organization's work output and building your market at the same time.

Your trade association can help advertise safety in much the same way as plastics manufacturers, dry cleaners, and government agencies banded together to prevent misuse of soft plastic bags.

3. You can also educate consumers by improving your point-of-sale activities. Whether your sales are through detail men, customer representatives, contact men, or people on the retail floor in your customer's store, teach them about the limitations of your product. Further, give them some exposure to product liability law and how it bears on their activities. The price of carelessness is high; they should know enough to avoid, by word or deed, creating a liability situation for you. They should be trained in demonstrating safety features, intelligent operation of the product, and how to prevent misuse and abuse. Literature should be available that will give the consumer meaningful information about the product. (Such literature is required by law for some products, such as automobiles.)

4. Finally, improve the box in which the product is packaged and the enclosures that come with the product. Manufacturers have an unfortunate tendency to make one instruction book cover all the models and options and not clearly label which features come on a particular model and which are options. The user has to wade through a sea of information, determine what does and does not pertain to his purchase, and apply his learning to the safe use of the product. Then manufacturers complain that "no one reads the instructions."

Toys should be packaged in boxes more suited to storage than to mere display, so that instructions and cautions on the inside cover are more likely to be retained. This practice will most assuredly run up packaging costs, but you should educate the consumer on the benefits of having a storage box for the item (i.e., the instructions won't get lost) and the fact that the instructions are written (where feasible) in language and terminology suited to the age of the child.

Educate the consumer to recognize symbols for poisons, high heat, and electricity hazard, and put them on the product as a constant reminder.

CONTINUOUSLY PREPARE FOR LIABILITY

A bad product will get through, and it may cause injury and damage. Expecting this to happen and preparing accordingly will lead to no surprises.

First, review your warranty situation. Beware of creating warranty conditions you do not intend to or cannot fulfill. Restrict your warranties with disclaimers or other precise limiting language; the courts will probably ignore them in cases of injury litigation, but you stand some chance of limiting consequential economic damages. Your attorney will probably make you put disclaimers not only in your contracts but in every piece of promotional or instructional literature.

The courts are in a state of flux. Some see no difference between an unconscionable limitation of responsibility for personal injury and an unconscionable limitation of responsibility for economic injury. Other courts follow the letter of the manufacturer's disclaimer. If his case had been tried in the latter type of court, the flower grower whose commercial beds were burned out would have found himself reimbursed with a new sack of fertilizer, if anything.

Be especially vigilant if you are selling to children while using magazine "seals" or endorsements to buttress your sales pitch to the parents. You may be creating one set of warranties between yourself and the children (depending on how they interpret your message) and leaving yourself open to additional attack if the "seal" has been awarded to anyone who simply advertises in the magazine.[12] And, as we discussed in an earlier chapter, don't advertise the product by having an expert do dangerous stunts with it.

Second, keep your information channels open to pick up failure trends and consumer complaints. There are in existence computer-driven systems that will track numbers of failures, will allow you to enter alphanumeric material explaining failures, and will retain, analyze, and print out the material in various formats. Make use of these to protect yourself against charges of being indifferent.

Third, keep your files well-organized, up to date, clear of misleading material, and pertinent to particular production runs. Don't sanitize them by eliminating records of failures of the designs sent into production. Explain the failures and the actions taken to prevent recurrence. Retain the files and your insurance policies indefinitely.

If records are to be microfilmed for long-term storage, an audit may be accomplished during the microfilming stage. The question of the legality of microfilm records is often raised. Kish [13] says that the question cannot be definitely answered, but the manager should keep in mind that federal courts will generally accept microfilm records if (1) the filming occurred in the normal course of business; and (2) the original records were photographed accurately, in their entirety, and legibly. Most states follow these guidelines in admitting microfilm records for evidence. Kish also recommends having the legal department fill out a certificate-of-authenticity form as the last item for every group of documents related to a particular matter and then microfilming the form along with the documents.

Fourth, keep your organization's liability-prevention team sharply honed. When a lawsuit occurs, get your hands on the product, interview witnesses to the event that caused the damage, and note the environment in which the product was functioning, the characteristics of those who were using it (education, training, etc.), and all other material which bears on the problem. Have your people do tests on the product and try to determine exactly what went wrong. If the product is not available, obtain one as close as possible to it and see what you can discover. It then may be advisable to call in an outside expert to buttress (or refute) your conclusions. If he does the latter, your pretrial preparation must be intensified to reconcile the differences that exist—or your attorney will move to settle the case, as discussed in Chapter 4.

CHANGE MANAGEMENT ATTITUDES

In 1970 the National Commission on Product Safety issued a devastating report about the carnage wrought by consumer products. Since then we have entered the age of consumerism. We have OSHA, the CPSC, the FTC, and dozens of agencies that make information on product safety available and lobby against unsafe products. The media give recalls top play. Insurance claims have ballooned, and deductibles running into six and seven figures are not infrequent.[14] Out-of-court settlements in the $50,000 range are not unusual, and legal defense costs are enormous.

How much of this has penetrated management's thinking? In 1970, Clarke complained that 60 percent of those manufacturers who voluntarily responded to a mail survey were carrying out safety work with no written safety policy.[15] Two-thirds, he said, reported they were using human-factors analyses, yet only a few percent had human-factors engineers to carry them out. In a 1972 article, Wise reported that three major manufacturing companies attributed 5 percent of their total 8 percent turnover in technical personnel to problems in the product liability area.[16] The explanation (according to Richard Jacobs): "When these engineers saw products being designed and produced that weren't acceptable to their own thinking, instead of knocking their heads against a brick wall trying to push management in the right direction, they gave up and quit." [17] In 1974, 2,000 industrial research managers responded to an opinion poll about product safety. Over 60 percent of the respondents knew of instances where changes in design were needed for product safety but were not made.[18] When asked how much attention was given to product safety considerations, 44 percent answered that it was poor or not quite adequate.

Management tends to equate quality with avoidance of problems, and the reward-punishment system of the firm encourages this attitude. It has taken "Big Brother," in the form of government agencies, to bludgeon safety consciousness into the executive mind. Add to that the poundings in the courtroom and maybe there will be some changes made.

Fostering the lack of movement is the fact that many firms have a distorted view of what a good quality control program will cost, versus their costs for insurance and claim settlement. Take insurance costs: In May 1970 Clarke reported, on the basis of manufacturers' questionnaire responses, that liability insurance costs were about 0.05 percent of sales.[19] Informal estimates later that year raised this figure, even with deductibles and exclusions, to not more than 1 percent. (By now the percentage may be slightly higher.) Firms take an instinctive position against expenditures for better quality control because, they feel, "claims are under control" and insurance is cheap compared to improving quality control.

Of course, as we saw in Chapter 5, claims are not necessarily under control. And another counter to this line of reasoning comes from Kidwell, a respected industry quality control spokesman. He found that in many firms the cost of quality control—because of defects, rework, and all other problems—was running as high as 10–12 percent of sales or 20–24 percent of manufacturing costs.[20] By contrast, in a properly run program the cost of quality should never be over 4 percent of sales or 8 percent of manufacturing costs.[21] The former figure is made up of the following elements:

Cost of planned quality control program: 2.5% of sales
Unplanned waste (including rework, scrap,
   and warranty):   1.5% of sales

For military or government work, Kidwell increases the costs of a planned quality control program to 3 percent of sales (and allows 2 percent for unplanned waste).

Kidwell recommends that since 4 percent (or 5 percent in military work) is an appropriate target for quality costs while in many firms it is probably closer to 10–12 percent, a quality "profit plan" should be made part of the business plan of the corporation. Only in this way will quality control achieve appropriate recognition for the costs it saves and the other benefits it can bring.

Crisis management, in which cases are handled on an ad hoc basis, leads to heavy pressures on middle-level managers and on engineers, but the real burden is on foremen. An organization under stress responds with centralization of control, centralization of decision making, and issuance of management fiats. All pretense of industrial democracy is lost as middle managers "report," engineers "respond," and the foreman bears the brunt of change pressures on the factory floor.[22] Considering the enormous burden already on the first-line supervisor, liability problems are sure to create new levels of alienation in this crucial area of a firm's personnel structure, to say nothing of its effects on the other groups mentioned. Since top management achieves its greatest successes with a motivated hierarchy performing in a systematized operating manner,[23] this is reason enough to avoid the ad hoc treatment of liability problems.

REMAIN CONTINUOUSLY ALERT TO CHANGING CONDITIONS

If you want to have an all-inclusive liability-prevention program, it is not sufficient to depend on your attorney to keep the firm up to date. The internal mechanisms of the firm must be charged with the responsibility as well. This takes the form of four major actions: intelligent complaint investigation, reading appropriate literature, staying current on the law, and working with meaningful code-making groups.

Intelligent Complaint Investigation

We have discussed the monitoring of complaints and the roles of various departments in regard to complaints. Now we will discuss how to use them to keep up to date.

First, on a macro level: We know that consumer complaints

reach Congress and the executive branch. They also reach organizations and consumer advocates who have influence with these government arms. The feelings of the electorate will eventually be translated into laws that not only will correct the abuses of the industrial few but will restrict the freedom to operate, and run up the costs, of the many. Those executives who find it hard to live with Section 15b of the CPSA (requires notification to government of a serious defect within 24 hours) have only to think of the serious abuses of the consumer's trust that brought such a law into being. When abuses perpetrated by your competitors surface, you cannot stand aloof and hope for corrections through the "invisible hand" of the marketplace. Products have become too complicated for Adam Smith's eighteenth-century theories to operate—especially with unsophisticated purchasers. Put some muscle into the trade association, and if necessary expel the abuser. If your association has demonstrated meaningful concern for safety and then takes such an action, the competitor might make some corrections—upon contemplating the potential impact of the expulsion in court and on his insurance underwriter. Above all, adopt an industry attitude that people are sincere in their complaints and that even their misuse and abuse of products, if repeated on a wide scale, are matters of legitimate concern to you. Educate the consumer, change the products, and, if absolutely necessary, withdraw them from the market. Passage of a law to right wrongs will not be necessary if your industry does everything it can to right them itself.

On a micro level, within your firm, computer printouts of complaints can quickly point out not only where the product is presently falling down but where future improvements are needed. In some cases, abuse of the product may show the way to an "industrial-version" or "heavy-duty" item with, possibly, better profit margins than the original. Accident investigations not only reveal explanations for past faults but offer keys to future improvements. Quality control personnel, who are oriented to production processes, will see an accident from a totally different perspective than would a safety engineer. The latter will suggest changes in the product; the former will suggest new methods of monitoring and controlling the way the product was built. The same divergency of viewpoints will be seen between designers and marketers, and in other divisions of the firm—provided that management does not bury its mistakes but rather leads the organization in learning from them.

A Reading Program

In the references at the end of Chapter 1 we gave some sources of product liability reports. Your attorney should funnel to you material he thinks appropriate to your operation, but don't depend solely on him. Only your engineers, for example, might be able to connect toxicity of a totally unrelated product with potential problems for you. All the departments in your firm should be exposed to the problems of other firms and other products, and be alerted to watch for their implications for your own product. The company library should subscribe to product liability reports just as it does to technical magazines.

Your attorney should also teach your people how to intelligently read court decisions, appeals motions, and rulings. In particular, they should learn to interpret a judge's opinion. Frequently, only a very small part of a judge's opinion deals with and decides the issues of a case. This is the material from which our body of case law evolves. The rest—i.e., anything not necessary to decide the issue of a case—is a form of judicial opinion called dicta.

Sometimes dicta are important, however. The courts use dicta as indicators of their thinking on matters related to the case, so reading them gives some indication of what the decisions might be if those matters arose. Thus, if a particular case has been decided on very narrow legal issues, read the dicta to find out if there are any criticisms of your operations, products, or firm in general that might come up again in a future case. View such criticisms as a "judicial consultant's" opinions of your firm, and note where improvements are needed.

The company library should assume an important role in keeping your engineers and scientists up to date and exposed to as broad a scope of developments as possible. One publication we recommend is the *Federal Register*. You may want to obtain individual subscriptions for key persons on the design-review team, for your top marketing and risk management people, and for your engineers. This journal will help you respond quickly to rule proposals on the part of federal agencies and will keep all levels of the organization up to date on regulatory thinking.

We also suggest a loose liaison with the local law school library. Law review articles make superb reading even for engineers, accountants, managers, and marketers. They are clearly written, are completely descriptive of the law and its background for virtually every issue discussed, and are excellent references for company internal publications and briefings. They are written by top-name judges and practicing attorneys as well as people in the academic world. Attorneys will sometimes get an advance indication of a judge's feelings from an article he or she wrote.

Staying Current on the Law

The much feared class-action suit has been considerably "defanged" by the Supreme Court rulings mentioned in Chapter 1. The Court ruled that (1) individual claims of a class cannot be pooled to meet the $10,000 minimum claim required before a federal court will hear the suit; and (2) all the people who can be identified must receive notice of the suit at the investigator's expense.[24] But you should still watch the activities of conservationists, pollution fighters, and groups concerned with industrial health. The legal tools evolved by these groups may bring back to life a revitalized class-action threat. Or Congress may pass enabling legislation to overcome the negative effects of the Supreme Court's decisions.

We expect that today's form of loss distribution will change. The deep-pocket theory—and the idea that companies can recover their costs through price and tax mechanisms—will be increasingly called into question. The higher prices, of course, are borne by the consumer. And many accident costs are absorbed by the consumer or other product owner out of his own pocket, through the costs of medical insurance, disability or compensation insurance, and property insurance. The fault and adversary systems we now have in the courts are extremely costly for witnesses, juries, and other participants and result in enormous, unreimbursed expenditures by plaintiffs or other injured parties.[25] Calabresi argues strongly that the fault system even does a miserable job of deterring decisions that lead to accidents. Decisions are often made by balancing the probable costs of liability suits (as they might affect the corporation through the insurance and tax mechanisms) against the actual cost of making the product safer. The fault system does not have the ingredients necessary to make unenlightened management weight the scales sufficiently on the side of a safer product; it is too often easier to go the route of betting on the insurance and tax mechanisms to keep costs down to an acceptable level. The fault system, Calabresi says, "pays little attention to which of the possible categories of cost bearers is most likely to be aware of the risk involved [in the use of a product]."[26] As a result, in any measurement of total costs versus total reimbursement, it is the injured party who comes out the heaviest loser. Thus, the fault system hurts most not the perpetrator of the decisions which led to the accident, but rather its victim.

By contrast, workmen's compensation laws have had a measurable impact on the safety of the workplace. The employer is liable for the accident regardless of who is at fault. The risks and accident costs can be easily compared with the costs of compensation insurance and the desired safety devices. Here the result has been, as Calabresi points out, that many safety devices have been adopted.[27] We see a movement toward some form of accident compensation on a no-fault basis coming into being, with insurers covering the product instead of the firm. The consumer or user would be paid on the basis of a schedule for loss of limbs, disability, and so forth, and the costs would be directly charged against the product. Using Calabresi's reasoning, this should result in the installation of safety devices or in safer products. In the context of keeping up to date, we see that management must begin instituting systems to remove legal and claims costs from general overhead to a more direct basis. You should prepare for the time when all the aforementioned agencies that are now absorbing many of your defect costs (such as medical insurers) pass them back to you in a new no-fault, "workmen's compensation" type of plan. Such a system would have the beneficial effect of costing a product more accurately on the firm's books.

Along the way to no-fault, we see the increased use of court-appointed technical experts, sometimes backed up with laboratory funds for more thorough investigation of the product. We may soon see a reduction in battles over qualifying witnesses, destruction of a case because of a plaintiff attorney's poor examination of his expert, and sleight of hand in the clarity of a chart or set of figures presented to the jury. The court expert will know as much about your product as you, will be empowered to visit your premise to fill in any gaps he has in his knowledge, and will not be shaken in court. He will be impartial, knowing no allegiances. The court decisions will begin to reflect his technical input, the issue decisions and the dicta will be more precisely focused on you and your industry, and you may well find yourself with a very expensive form of operations audit.

With regard to changes in legal theories per se, we see the following major development. Standard liability theory holds the manufacturer responsible for injuries caused by design defects unless the product was misused and abused. But what about cases where the design defect, instead of causing the injury, simply made the injury (or damage sustained) much worse? The courts have split on this issue. Ten states and the District of Columbia have ruled that the manufacturer is liable; eleven states have held that he is not.[28] Legislation may be needed to resolve this issue, and there is no reason to expect that it will provide an easy out for the manufacturer. On the contrary, manufacturers may well have to run more intensive (and expensive) tests-to-destruction to prove that the design defect could not have aggravated the injury in question.

Working with Code-Making Groups

The new, court-appointed experts will have to draw their standards from somewhere—which leads us to reemphasize the importance of code- or standard-setting groups. Giving heavy company support to these groups is as intelligent a "capital investment" as buying a new inspection device. Your company's aim should be not only to protect its own interests but to come out with a standard that won't be an industry whitewash. Bend your product to meet the standard, not vice versa. If you do end up in court, the combination of a well-made product, an impartial engineer, and a high standard that you met when the product was designed will give you a very strong defense. And aside from the question of legal defense, when you sit down with your insurer to discuss next year's rates, the standard may well be the strongest document you produce to prove that you installed all available safety devices or took all available safety precautions.

CONCLUSION

Top management must constantly monitor and take an interest in "the state of the firm" in preventing product liability If the firm truly expects to move away from the crisis approach to product defects and their consequences, quality must receive appropriate recognition in tradeoffs with quantity and cost. We come back to the considerations mentioned in Chapter 1: Don't circumscribe quality control activities, do build in product liability prevention through better products, and above all, accept control of the product itself as a major management responsibility. This means that all activities related to the product must be audited, and the reward-punishment system must recognize liability prevention as a legitimate method of increasing the firm's profits and keeping company people out of the courtroom or jail.

You may even wind up with more satisfied customers—and that is the real name of the game.

REFERENCES

1. F. Reed Dickerson, ed., *Product Safety in Household Goods* (Indianapolis: Bobbs-Merrill, 1968), p. 89.

2. "The Lead in Canada's Electric Teakettles," *Business Week* (June 8, 1974), p. 27.
3. Ibid.
4. Joann S. Lublin, "Time Bombs: Old Treatments' Risks Spur Wide Searches for Former Patients," *The Wall Street Journal* (June 4, 1974), p. 1.
5. "NHTSA Seeks Information from the Public," *Quality Management and Engineering* (June 1974), p. 11.
6. Carl C. Clarke, "Safety System Dynamics for Consumer Products —Some Factors Affecting Decisions About Safety." 21st Annual Appliance Technical Conference, Institute of Electrical and Electronic Engineers, Mansfield, Ohio, May 5, 1970. Published in *The American Society of Safety Engineers Journal* (October 1970), pp. 17–23.

     See also *Design of a Statistical Information System for Product Related Injuries*, Document PB194871 (Springfield, Va.: National Technical Information Service, U.S. Department of Defense, 1970); and the following, all published in 1970 by the Cornell Aeronautical Laboratory, Inc. (now Calcomp), Buffalo, New York 14221: (1) "A Study of the Cost Involved for Improved Quality Control of Carbonated Beverages in One Way Bottles," Contract 70-164, CAL Report VZ-2926-D-1, (2) "A Study of the Cost of Safety Innovations in Consumer Products," CAL Report VZ-2926-D-5, (3) "Cost to the Consumer of Improving the Safety of Consumer Products," CAL Report VZ-2926-D-3.
7. "FDA Reporting Systems Track Down Unsafe Products," *Quality Progress* (February 1973), p. 43.
8. "Dictating Product Safety," *Business Week* (May 18, 1974), p. 70.
9. National Safety Council, Chicago, Illinois. When completed there will be 16 volumes of checklists.
10. Clarke, op. cit., p. 5.
11. Ibid.
12. See Edward M. Swartz, *Toys That Don't Care* (Boston: Gambit, 1971), Chapter 4.
13. Joseph L. Kish, Jr., "The Legality of Microfilm Records," *Business Graphics* (August 1974), pp. 30–31.
14. "The Rising Cost of Liability Claims," *Business Week* (March 9, 1974), p. 50.
15. Clarke, op. cit., p. 7.
16. Clare E. Wise, "Carnage in the Courtroom," *Machine Design* (May 4, 1972), p. 22.

17. Richard M. Jacobs, quoted in ibid.
18. "Product Safety at Any Cost," *Industrial Research* (May 1974), p. 83.
19. Clarke, op. cit., p. 12.
20. John L. Kidwell, "Impact of Quality on Profits," *Fourteenth Annual Symposium Transactions* (Milwaukee, Wisc.: American Society for Quality Control, 1970), p. 17.
21. Ibid.
22. James G. March, ed., *Handbook of Organizations* (Chicago: Rand McNally & Company, 1965), Chapter 25.
23. Ibid., p. 1093.
24. "High Court Curbs Suits on Behalf of Large Group," *The New York Times*, May 29, 1974, p. 1.
25. Guido Calabresi, *The Costs of Accidents* (New Haven, Conn.: Yale University Press, 1970), Chapter 14.
26. Ibid., p. 244.
27. Ibid., p. 245.
28. "Auto Liability Split," *Business Week* (June 8, 1974), p. 98.

INDEX

A

accidents, 33-37
  industrial, 88
accreditation groups, product safety, 182
administrative law, 25
administrative regulations, 15
advertising and consumer education, 214-215
American Baking Institute, 3n
American Law Institute, 22
American National Standards Institute (ANSI), 179, 182
American Society of Mechanical Engineers, 6
American Society for Quality Control, 6

Apollo 13, explosion of, 5
appeals courts
  functions of, 118
  trends in, 118
attorney
  defense, 73-76
    aim of, 96
    analysis of case by, 76-93
    building of case by, 73-93
    choice of, 76
    and interrogatory, 85
    preparedness of, 135
    in semi-rural area, 98
  plaintiff, 37-43
    and bill of particulars, 58-59
    building of case by, 32-65
    choice of, 96
    and choice of engineer, 54-55

jury
    charge to, 117
    importance in liability cases,
        53
    investigation of, 104
    reaction to sampling, 48
    selection of, 103-105
    size of, 103-104
    and voir dire, 103

K

Karrass, Chester L., 95
Kidwell, John L., 219-220

L

labeling, *see* warning
Labor Department, 155
law, 15
    administrative, 25
    case, 16
    statutory, 15
    workmen's compensation, 224
lawsuits, company attitude to-
        ward, 72-73
lawyer, *see* attorney
Lawyers Desk Reference, 39, 43
layer concept, and liability ac-
        tion, 70-71
liability
    continuous preparation for,
        216-218
    contractual, 130
    of manufacturer, 75
    "sistership," 129
    under tort, 21

liability-prevention system
    administration of, 185-202
    audit documents, 174-183
        board-of-directors audits,
            175-176
        external certification, 178-
            179
        staff audits, 176-178
    and code-making groups,
        225-226
    and defense team, 201-203
    departmental roles, 189-197
        field engineering and main-
            tenance, 196-197
        manufacturing, 193
        marketing, 194-195
        personnel, 193-194
        product engineering, 192-
            193
        purchasing, 196
        research and design, 192
    design review, 187-189
    development of, 159-160
    executive role, 186-187
    genealogy-tracing docu-
        ments, 183-185
    inspection, 169
    management attitude toward,
        218-220
    performance documents, 160-
        174
        change-control-procedures
            manual, 163-164
        checklists, 165-172
        customer relations manual,
            173-174
        drafting-standards manu-
            al, 161-162